NOVELS BY JD BUZZARD

THE ELITE SAGA (YOUNG ADULT)

THE ELITE (RETIRED)

GEN3: ORIGIN OF THE ELITE

HEAVENS RAIN HELL: BATTLE OF THE ELITE

RISE OF THE ELITE: EVIL RISES

CHILDREN BOOKS BY JD BUZZARD

THE 1st BIG BOOK of CHILDREN's TOPICS of QUALITY

THE 2nd BIG BOOK of CHILDREN's TOPICS of QUALITY

CHILDREN'S TOPICS of QUALITY SERIES

MAKING THE RIGHT CHOICE BOOK 1: THE JOURNEY of ADVENTURES with CHOICES

MAKING THE RIGHT CHOICE BOOK 2: THE JOURNEY to SMART CHOICES

MAKING THE RIGHT CHOICE BOOK 3: THE JOURNEY to CHOICES THROUGH MUSIC

MAKING THE RIGHT CHOICE BOOK 4: THE JOURNEY to FIND RESPONSIBILITIES & EMPOWERMENT

MAKING THE RIGHT CHOICE BOOK 5: THE JOURNEY to FIND EMPATHY, STRENGTH & COMPASSION

MAKING THE RIGHT CHOICE BOOK 6: THE JOURNEY to ACCEPTANCE

MAKING THE RIGHT CHOICE BOOK 7: THE JOURNEY to THINKING

MAKING THE RIGHT CHOICE BOOK 8: THE JOURNEY of NAVIGATING SOCIAL SKILLS

MAKING THE RIGHT CHOICE BOOK 9: THE JOURNEY to SAVE the PLANET

MAKING THE RIGHT CHOICE BOOK 10: THE JOURNEY to WISE SPENDING

Thoughts on Quality, Business & Life

A Collection from Experience

JD BUZZARD

Thoughts on Quality, Business & Life
A Collection from Experience

Sale of this book without a front cover may be unauthorized. If this book is coverless, it may have been reported to the publisher as "unsold or destroyed" and neither the author nor the publisher may have received payment for it.

Copyright © 2024 by JD Buzzard. All Rights Reserved.

External Cover art is thanks to (freepik on Freepik.com).
Internal Cover art is thanks to (Racool_studio on Freepik.com)
Internal art is thanks to (freepik, rawpixel.com, vectorjuice, gpointstudio, pch.vector, yanalya, 8photo, creativeart, jcomp, upklyak, juicyfish, pressfoto, macrovector, wirestock, pikisuperstar, redgreystock on Freepik.com)

First Edition (Paperback): (Dec 2024)

All rights reserved. The text of this publication, or any part thereof, may not be reproduced in any manner whatsoever without written permission from the publisher.

The characters and events in this book are fictitious. Any similarity to real persons, living or dead, is coincidental and not intended by the author.

ISBN: (9798339708223)

Printed in the United States of America

10 9 8 7 6 5 4 3 2 1

To Everyone Out There

Often, we must learn things the hard way. I would like to help with that as lessons learned is something to share, both positive and negative.

A word from the author…

As you read through this you will see similar themes as whether you are at work, home, or out in public, you will find certain aspects in life will impact us everywhere at any time. This book does not have to be read cover to cover, as you can jump around to whatever topics you wish to read about.

These various thoughts throughout this book cover some of what I have posted across social media over the last two years since I decided to start putting my experience to use in order to help people wherever they are.

Having worked over thirty years in more than one country and more than one field, I have learned a lot from others and sometimes through difficult times.

Having been working since before I was a teenager, like many of my generation has, I have seen and done a lot in a shorter amount of time than others in the workforce.

Having been a trainer in every job I have had since my teenage years, I have learned how to teach, coach, educate, and mentor individuals and teams. Much of that was through learning myself, along with growth and time to get to where I could achieve positive results.

Having children, I wanted to be able to give what I have learned to both the younger generation as well as anyone interested in learning a little something. I am always reading, learning, and studying a wide variety of subjects because I enjoy it. I also listen, which is very important to those who wish to learn.

No matter how old we get in life, there is something to do, something to learn, and something to teach. Even if we are fortunate to retire in good health, staying active will keep you healthier longer.

For the younger generations, often free time is spent on phones, social media, television, games, but not in learning about subjects they can use through both school and work life.

In addition to this book of thoughts, I have a collection of children books on a variety of topics that teaches children to make decisions based on integrity, accountability, honesty, with ethical, intelligent & empathic thought & critical thinking. These are skills that everyone can use throughout their life. Learning while you are young, makes it easier and it becomes a part of our lives where we then don't have to worry about that for adults entering the workforce.

Each person on this planet is unique, with a unique environment. Each person on this planet learns differently. Giving every person on this planet an opportunity to learn in their way, with subjects small to big, makes this planet and its inhabitants a stronger, more intelligent and overall better place to live.

Let's try together.

Contents of Thoughts on Quality, Business & Life

Introduction

Part 1: Quality

Chapter 1- Why Start with Quality? What is Quality, Why Does It Matter & Why it is Important?
Chapter 2- Levels of Importance
Chapter 3- Change Management
Chapter 4- Processes
Chapter 5- Preventing Problems
Chapter 6- Quality Assurance & Quality Control
Chapter 7- Requirements Known & Met
Chapter 8- Nonconformity
Chapter 9- Cost of Quality: Value Add & Non-Value Add
Chapter 10- Improvements
Chapter 11- Quality Culture & Buy In
Chapter 12- Keys to Working Quality
Chapter 13- Explaining Quality

Part 2: Business

Chapter 1- Responsibility
Chapter 2- Leadership
Chapter 3- Planning & Structure
Chapter 4- Experts, Ambition, Motivation & Vision
Chapter 5- What is Important & the Goal?
Chapter 6- Communication & Skills
Chapter 7- Ego, Confidence & Emotional Intelligence
Chapter 8- Understanding the Team & Teamwork
Chapter 9- Delegating
Chapter 10- Trust & Relationships
Chapter 11- Accountability & Integrity
Chapter 12- Loyalty & Transparency
Chapter 13- Toxicity
Chapter 14- Finances
Chapter 15- Words Matter
Chapter 16- Solving Problems
Chapter 17- Flexibility
Chapter 18- Feedback, Disagreements & Defensiveness

Chapter 19- Reports & KPI's
Chapter 20- Technology
Chapter 21- Meetings
Chapter 22- Time Management

Part 3: Life

Chapter 1- Empathy
Chapter 2- A Gift to Yourself and Others
Chapter 3- Boundaries
Chapter 4- Time, Time to Unplug & Value
Chapter 5- Frustration, Stress & Burnout
Chapter 6- Perception & Fear
Chapter 7- Learning
Chapter 8- Making Everyone Happy
Chapter 9- Jumping to Conclusions & Personal Issues
Chapter 10- Honesty

Closing

INTRODUCTION

Welcome to my thoughts. Dangerous, yes.

Back when kids could, I started my work life delivering newspapers each day before I was even a teenager. I juggled that while in school and moved into the back of a fast food kitchen for a Christmas season before moving into retail for a few years. All while doing this I continued to juggle school, volunteer activities & other side jobs year long.

I started training and mentoring others during my teenage years while working in retail. I also did it in my volunteer time and when I worked as a sound engineer as one of my side gigs.

By the end of my teenage years I reached burnout before it was a popular word as it is today. All those years though were formulative to my future work ethic.

My next career was working mail where I continued to learn, to teach, and to take the lead when allowed. That eventually gave me the opportunity to expand my abilities by taking my knowledge and expertise oversees where I conquered a new environment.

While in this environment I continued to learn while I also taught and led others. Here is where I began to learn about Quality and brought it into the workplace. This is where I began to plan for the next chapter in my career which would lead me to move into Quality full time.

When I was in my teenage years, I would often feel the animosity of those older around me because of my age and ability. Now that I am a bit older, I understand that. While there may be prodigies that quickly gain excellence in their field or art, often it takes time. It can take many years working in a field before you become an expert.

Even with my years working, there are and have been those around me that have twenty more years than me because of age. I have known people that have been in a field longer than I have been alive. It is difficult to counter that in discussions because the one with the years tend to trump those without.

My goal with this book is to bring ideas to the forefront of the minds of those who are interested in absorbing them. I have gathered a decent sized group of followers, connections and acquaintances across social media and work life where we feed off each other's knowledge. My goal when I started posting on social media was to pass along knowledge as well as learn from others.

If you want to join me in that, stop by and say hi. I hope that the thoughts in the forthcoming pages will help you at work, home and out in the world.

Part 1
Quality

Chapter 1
Why Start with Quality?
What is Quality, Why Does It Matter & Why is it Important?

Why do I start with Quality in this 3-part book? Simply put, everything in both business and our personal lives starts with Quality, even if we may not realize it.

  Quality is in the eye of the beholder. In business it is the customer or client who drives what quality is for them. Even though business executives may consider other aspects of their business as important or come first in their eyes, like finances or safety, without starting with quality the other aspects will not be in line with requirements first. Long term this will have a negative impact on a business that does not focus on quality to build their business on as a foundation business system.
  Regardless if a business is interested in quality related certifications, not having quality in mind will erode what the business has in place.

A foundation, metaphorically or physical, needs to be built on a solid foundation, which when implemented correctly, is Quality.

Next are some thoughts on the importance of Quality, in no particular order.

It is important that process owners and leaders take ownership and responsibility for the quality standard in their function. They drive for success, not a quality team if there even is one.

This may be divisive, but from a Quality standpoint it can be a serious concern.

Quality is meant to be independent, when there is an actual Quality team within a business. Many businesses do not have Quality and utilize others in the role as a secondary task. The right people need to be in the right role for anything, to include Quality.

That is not what this topic is about. If there is a Quality team they are meant to be independent from all other functional departments as they are the team who ensures everyone is on point with requirements, plus more.

From an International Organization of Standardization (ISO) standpoint, if a company wishes to be certified or compliant to an ISO standard, Quality answers only to the top.

A concern though is even with that chain of command, if the top leadership is controlling the Quality team to the point where they are hindered or not able to do their job as they feel is needed, they are not truly independent and possibly a puppet or figure head department.

The capability is stunted and the various aspects of Quality within the company may certainly be damaged with the lack of proper oversight.

Something to think about for those interested in a creating a strong Quality Culture where everyone is striving to do their best for the client/customer while continually improving what they do every day.

Top down/bottom up throughout the organization needs to be involved, interested and supportive of the initiative to be better today than you (we) were yesterday and better tomorrow than you (we) are today.

Too often you will hear we have to get this done, and right now.

That is often used to bypass requirements within a process because time is of the essence.

Incorrect.

Any process needs to take account of time, risk, potential issues and as many variables as possible. Doing it correctly, the way intended for the client/customer, is critical.

Don't get rushed into making errors because it will backfire and there are too many examples of this happening and people dying because of it.

Lessons are meant to be learned, history retained and used to prevent reoccurrence.

You can work smarter and not harder and any process is living and can be improved upon. That is one of the functions of Quality, to work with leaders and process owners to improve it.

Do what is right, even when no one is looking.

Why should Quality be an independent department within a company?

I have seen where this was not the case, that they were ingrained within a department/function and/or answered to a lower lever position in the company.

To be successful a Quality department needs to answer to the highest level in the company.

If a company is interested in ISO certification this is important but besides that, only top management can drive Quality and positive change across the company.

Quality should not be directly involved in the creation of the product or service.

Conflict of interest is the issue. You want Quality to be impartial and objective with what they are looking at.

Now a hot topic that is often an issue within Quality is how deep to go with assistance.

Normally it is not Quality's position to do something for a given department, just advice through their audit findings and assist with process improvements, customer interaction and nonconformance findings to name a few.

Even the best of leaders cannot write a process. Not everyone has that strength.

Some companies will have Quality assist with the process development to meet the client/customer requirements.

Some will have Quality simply write it.

In the end what is important is that everyone agrees on the final solution/process which is in the best interest of meeting the client/customers' requirements.

Quality just ensures that the process is implemented and is working once in place.

Teamwork is essential in this, not divisiveness.

I have heard the phrase, Quality is a necessary evil, be invoked by folks on the past.

That mindset is completely wrong and detrimental to a company. It treats Quality as unimportant and something extra not valued.

Quality is generally what the client/customer expects. With that said, if a company doesn't take Quality seriously and invest in it, they won't have many clients/customers in the long run.

Quality should not be a pariah at work. They should be allowed to counsel/train/build systems and relationships, utilized to ensure a business is doing what they should be doing, what is right, helping to identify what isn't right and fixing it with process owners and finding ways to improve the company and its bottom line by making it more efficient.

Use them, don't shun them.

There are certain things within a Quality Management System that is important and those in leadership need to understand and nurture.

Some below and not in any order:

- Cost of Quality. Yes, factoring in Quality into your costs is important. It does cost some money, but it will cost more if you don't have Quality at all, and poor Quality will cost you more in the long term even if you don't realize it at first.
This can also include investing in technology that make the business more efficient. Improvements should be continuous.

- Training of Quality. Quality, like Safety, is everyone's responsibility. While folks in the operation may not be experts in Quality, they should have some basic ideas about it as they play a part in its success.

- Having Employee Buy In. Leadership needs to be on board first, but they need to ensure all employees understand the system and its intent. Why do they need to care? Why is it important?

- Be Proactive and not Reactive to everything. Stop putting out fires. Prevent them from occurring in the first place.

- Design your processes to what is needed and being done. Don't make them behind a desk alone. Get everyone involved. Don't make stuff up. Gear it to your Client/Customer requirements.

- Track what you need in order to be successful. Do you have everything in place to be truly successful? Resources.

- Review what you are doing internally to ensure you are successful for your client/customer. Don't wait on them to tell you. It could be too late if they bring up something negative that sours the relationship. Don't wait on Quality don't identify issues. Raise them to leadership. Fix, don't hide issues.

- Track change and communicate when change happens. It can affect any number of things in the workplace.

- Communication is essential and must be used efficiently. Get out of silos at work.

- Reduce single point failure opportunities at best as possible.

Take pride in your work.

The goal of Quality, besides meeting or exceeding the client/customer requirements in an efficient and compliant manner, is to assist the operational functions of a business by adding value.

You want to get bang for your buck, so to speak, and Quality can assist in driving towards Operational Excellence.

Utilize Quality when you can to get better at what you do.

A Quality System, regardless of its design and implementation, takes everyone's involvement in the business to be successful. Without that involvement, along with transparency and accountability, cracks will appear that could lead the business down a path no one should want. Let's work together to make Quality an important element in our daily lives.

Summary

While there may be important aspects to a business of any size, without incorporating Quality and treating it as important, those aspects will often fall short.

Quality is the foundation to build from and as such is something not to be overlooked.

In an ideal world, Quality is something that is a part of what you do in a company, not something extra. Some businesses and industries may have more leeway with requirements than others. If the customer or client gives you a set of requirements to follow, or there are government regulations, ignoring these for the sake of meeting timelines, deadlines and the mission, will cause long term failures that could cost you far more than doing it right the first time.

If you are fortunate to have a Quality team, use them wisely, and to your benefit, not to ignore or cover up issues. Use their ability and knowledge to help you be a better workplace.

Chapter 2
Levels of Importance

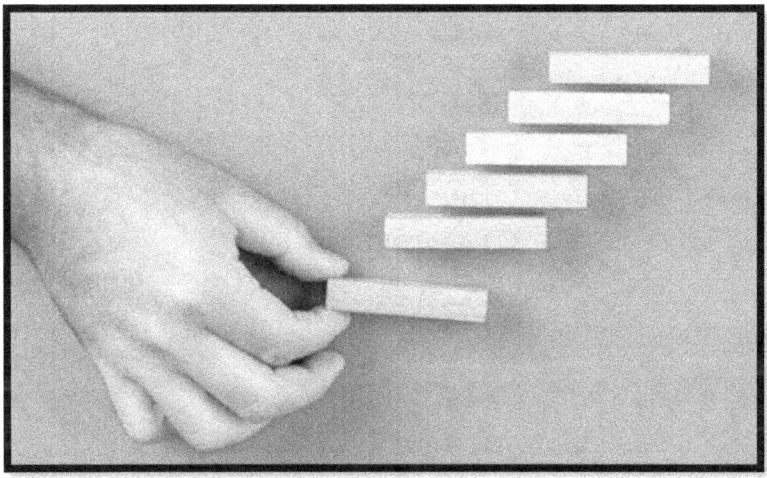

What is important in a business?

That is for the Sr. Leaders and executives to determine. What is their goal, their vision? What is the purpose of the company? What is important to them will be their focus.

While Quality is often not the focus, it is the aspect of the company that will determine how they achieve their customer/clients' requirements and needs. If Quality is not important, the business may achieve some success, but they will very rarely achieve the type of success that will advance them in their customer/clients' minds, and certainly not in others.

Next are some thoughts on importance, in no particular order.

It is important not to make a mountain out of a molehill when it comes to both work and home life.

There will times where we feel something is a bigger deal than it really is. We either exaggerate the situation or have a view that may not capture the entirety of it or long-term view. Will this be a problem a week, month or year from now?

We shouldn't allow a perceived problem cloud our eyes from what is really important, which could be those around us.

From a quality standpoint, we review potential nonconformities for levels of severity and impact to the customer, client and business itself.

It is important that we look at them with unbiased eyes and treat them as they really are and not go overboard with efforts.

It is also important to look at the big picture, with time, effort and who will be involved in writing a corrective action report and the tasks needed to correct and prevent long term.

Treat simple issues with simple problems and use resources where and when needed for the big issues that arise, if they do.

Always strive for excellence in what you do, but as we are all humans, there will be times we slip up.

Don't punish yourself or others with nonconformances. Look at the process first and treat nonconformances as improvement opportunities.

There will be nonconformities due to on purpose, ill-conceived actions, granted. That though should not be the initial assumption prior to a review, because the process can let us down.

Level of Effort.

Will the output equal or better than the input?

Is the effort even needed? If it isn't required for a client/customer or other requirement, is it value added?

What is the purpose behind the effort? Why is it needed? What all is required to exert? How much time and money will it cost?

It is important to know all this when deciding and planning a project/exercise/task.

You can take this into your personal life as well. It isn't just relegated to work.

I often hear from Leaders that they don't understand Quality. Prior to moving to Quality full time many years ago I learned about it and engrained it in my work location.

Quality, like Safety, should be something all leaders as well as all employees understand and ensure is in place.

We all want to go home in one piece and safely, but we should be working to ensure we are meeting our customer/clients requirements, internal requirements and finding ways to improve what we do and how we do it.

Leadership is the driving force behind a Quality and Safety minded workforce.

Encouraging Quality in the workplace will create a system of excellence that will drive future business. Keeping Quality out of decisions will, in the long term, have a negative impact on a business.

Summary

What is considered important will be different for each company and for each person within. There will rarely be a right answer, but my only argument is that especially for the mid to larger sized companies, Quality is looked at as a needed and important function. Quality is not a throw away word or to be ignored completely.

Quality, Safety, IT Security/Physical Security, Environmental, Human Resources, Finances and more all play a part in what we do each day. As a leader especially, it is vital to understand these various aspects and incorporate it into your daily tasks. Not doing so will leave you with holes/gaps that may bite you in the future.

What you consider to be your daily task alone may be the primary goal but is not the only goal to achieve.

Chapter 3
Change & Change Management

Change is constant in our lives. Sometimes it feels like it is constant while other times it slows down. There may be times change can become too much to handle. Whether at work, in our personal lives or out in the world, change happens.

We may lose our job, plunging us into an uncertain world. Our job may change or something at work changes, causing uneasiness and difficulties. Relationships in our lives may change, both positive and negative. Out in the world, a place we have enjoyed eating at, or shopping at may close, changing our habits.

It is on us how we adapt, which may take time and can be painful. Each person will handle change and the stress it may cause, differently, which is understandable. No matter what some may say, there is no one size fits all solution. Advice can be given, some good, some not as much, but it is on everyone on how they wish to take it and use it.

Next is a set of thoughts I have posted previously on social media regarding change. It is up to us alone on how we handle change, the advice we take and steps we take to go with the ebb and flow of life. Change can be the start to something great if we wish it to be. While not all change is desired or wanted at the time, positives can still be taken from it, even for less than desirable situations. This may take some time to discover, as time is often needed to move away from the change to see the bigger picture.

Change.

At any stage in our lives, whether work related or personal, it is rarely easy.

Regardless if the change is known, planned for and positive, there may still be apprehension.

I have heard a wide gambit of opinions on change. From "as long as it planned it is good," to "I hate change" and everything in between.

How each person handles change is different. You cannot expect everyone to feel as you do. And a change for one person may not be treated the same as another.

Promotions can still be difficult, even if positive, because it brings unknowns.

Changes in the workplace with new leadership or changes to work structure/tasks can bring uncertainty and stress.
New and sometimes extra workload may be beneficial to learn from, but will take time to learn, and in the meantime can be stressful.

Changes in relationships through loss or even gains can bring about unknown events and emotions in our lives.

These can be both positive and negative. In any case, change happens all the time in small and big ways and we must do our best to handle them.

We may not always like it, but we can face them in our own way. One answer or method will not fit all.

Building a business system takes effort and there are no quick fixes to implement. While there are plenty of great ideas to use for whatever you want to do, whether for Quality, Safety, Finance, HR, IT, Supply and more within a business, it takes buy in, understanding and time to get going.

Whether hiring a manager/director to implement or a consultant/coach, it comes down to support for the initiative.

Whatever the system, it needs to be designed for the company, easy to manage and easy to understand.

If the employees, let alone leadership, does not get it, it will be a failure.

Clear communication that occurs often with clear guidelines and outcomes for everyone involved is a must.

Change is not easy and muddled processes and actions will certainly not help.

Change may need to be implemented in stages to make transitions easier. Small steps are better than none.

In the world around us, change is usually the only constant.

Many businesses across the world have been through difficult times and their employees are impacted by this.

When a company goes through massive layoffs, the remaining employees are often expected to move on as though nothing happened. That rarely is the case.

While leadership may expect those remaining to be happy they still remain, there will be apprehension and often trust is lost.

If it happens once, it can happen again.

Morale will take a hit, and the companies image could be tarnished.

It is important that leaders lead, have open communication and set realistic expectations for those who remain, while also supporting outgoing employees.

It is rarely an easy time for all involved, at least those with empathy and a heart.

Positive change initiatives at work can make a business stronger, more profitable and even a healthier workplace. But many changes fail due to a number of issues.

- There has to be leadership buy in, in order for it to flow down to all employees.

- Failure to properly plan changes and manage it.

- Failure to communicate change to the workforce.

- Lack of clear requirements and outcomes needed by employees.

- Unorganized and not enough resources to make the change happen.

Don't set up employees to fail. It hurts the employees, morale, image of leadership and the company. Work to succeed on good change.

Even though we don't want to believe it, there are people who will never change.

This goes for work and personal life.

We want and hope someone will turn around, change their behavior, but there are some people who will remain in that rut.

At work, no matter how much we want to improve something, change the business and processes for the better, there will be some who will not confirm to the new idea. Doesn't matter if it is better, they are stuck in their ways and mindset.

There will be those around us as family, friends, neighbors who may have issues you want to address and fix with them. As much as we have good intentions, they may not reciprocate and push us away.

We may want to help and, in our minds, we shouldn't want to give up, but understand that they may not want help. That can be difficult to grasp and accept.

We should do our best each day to make those around us, to include ourselves, better. We all impact each other and it should be a positive impact. There is too much negative in the world to want to perpetuate it.
It shouldn't be considered a weakness to want to care.

Fear is a powerful force in our lives that will often hold us back from a change we may very well know will help us. Don't let fear control your life. It is too short as is to waste it on fear.

Some change is needed, while other change is brought on without our say.

Some change is good, while some is not so good.

Often an obstacle to change is ourselves which is needed to move ourselves forward.

Change isn't always easy of course, but it is needed from time to time.

You can't change your life until you change your life.

Seems pretty straight forward, but how easy is it?

There may be things you need to work on and there may be things you want to change that are easier said than done.

You won't know until you try. Making an effort, a true effort, even small will get you moving in the right direction.

This can apply to a business as well in how it operates for the client/customer requirements.

We all have something we can work on, whether at work or in our personal lives (maybe both), if we are true to ourselves.

Change happens all the time in small to big ways within our lives, whether at work or in our personal lives.

Some is good and should be embraced, while others throw a curve ball and is perceived as negative.

Change for the sake of change is rarely warranted or wanted/needed. On the other side of that coin, positive change, even in small steps, can make a workplace more efficient and into a 'work smarter and not harder situation'.

Change in the workplace to be successful should be planned and controlled, otherwise there could be chaos which can create a hostile environment. Communication is also a big part to this.

While it is good to be agile with change, that should be the exception and not the standard.

I have seen and continue to see plenty of leaders who don't like change even when it is good change. They are stuck in the *it's always been done that way mentality*.

In recent years a lot of change has leaned towards the negative and not positive. It feels as though we have taken many steps backwards in many cases.

When there is a change at work for a customer or client requirement, there should be a discussion and a process update. Training on the change is then done.

Identified process improvements can bring about positive change.

There should be more positivity in the workplace than negativity.

Change occurs in our work lives and personal lives, but in business it is important to get buy in from leadership and the employees that will be involved.

Change Acceleration Process (CAP) is a method with tools that can help facilitate this change discussion. Created 30+ years ago by General Electric, it is still a relevant way to see change be successful within a business. You can find CAP slides and tools across the web.

It is important to know and understand the change, what it takes to implement and ensure it sticks.

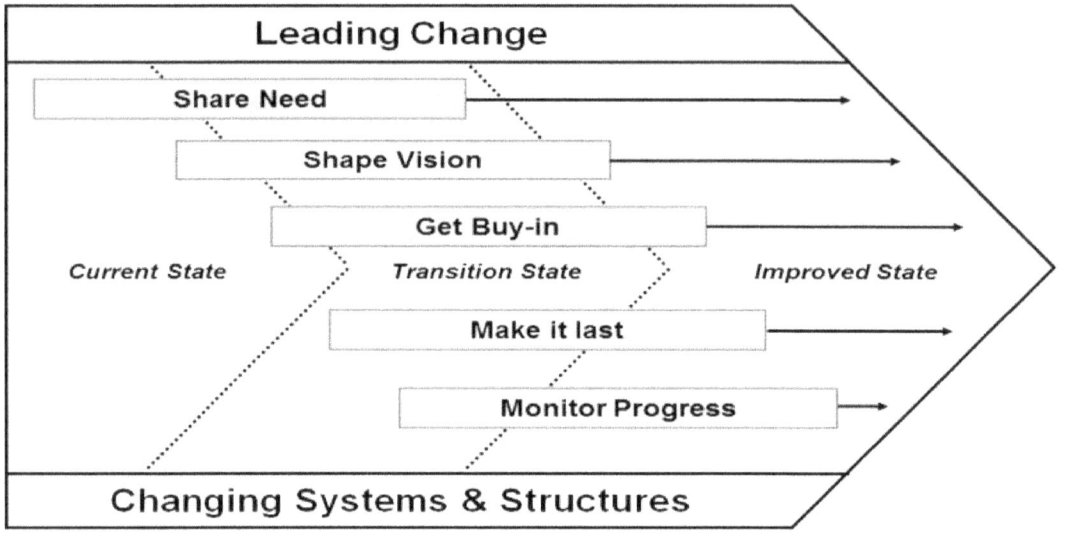

Chart example from 6 sigma inst.

Change happens in our personal lives and at work. At work there should be a controlled method to enact change. Short term, one-time change should be kept at a minimum for the welfare of the employees in the workplace to reduce chaos.

Continual improvement is also looked at which isn't always easy as people get used to the way things are done and doesn't feel it can be done better. Believe me it can, even in small ways.

It's important to be open to change. Not all change is negative or difficult. There is plenty of positive change to be had.

Summary

While change is not easy in a business, it is a part of it. Change needs to be handled the right way to have the right impact. If all the players involved are not a part of reviewing the change, the implementation will be terrible and probably will not succeed. Discussions need to be had with the team, understood and communicated. The initial change may require some revisiting for further improvements because often a roll out of a change does not quite go as planned and needs to be either redone or scrapped and a new plan started.

Not every idea will go perfectly once put into practice.

In the end change management within a company is often underutilized, ignored and not implemented correctly. It is important that this get turned around in order for a company to truly succeed.

Chapter 4
Processes

For a business to be successful, whether they are interested in Quality related certification or not, there needs to be something documented in place for employees to use when they need to use it.

Now this will widely change across the various sectors of work around the world. I didn't have anything documented to work from or pull out of a drawer for the first almost twenty years of my working life. It was all verbal.

Each company will be different, what they do is different, and their customer/client expectations are different. How they document their requirements to be met through continual, compliant outcomes, is up to them.

It should always be done in a manner easy for employees at any level to understand. Regardless of experience and education, it is important to have something written to rely on as we are all fallible and we will forget something from time to time.

Next are some of my thoughts on Processes, in no particular order.

Processes.

Some love them, some hate them.

Almost thirty years ago when I started in Food Service & Retail, there were no processes. It was on the job training and maybe some safety videos. When I became the trainer, I trained from experience.

When I moved into Postal twenty years ago, again there were no processes. I watched some safety videos and went to work.

Over the years, especially as customers/clients continually expect certain things a certain way in a Quality manner, processes have become important in some fields and businesses to ensure employees have a standard way to do things.

Over the last 15+ years I have written dozens upon dozens of processes, mainly as work instructions, manuals, Standard Operating Procedures (SOPs), Plans, etc., which also was used to build training slides. It has always been easier to have something to rely on and utilize for the workforce as many companies are in a dynamic workspace with many moving parts.

This is important is a business wants to be ISO certified. Documentation is the main piece ISO certifiers/registrars look for.

Experience and knowledge still matter, but I have heard many times from many leaders in companies that they don't require processes because they have experienced professionals. That is great, but people are fallible, and we are all not perfect and many companies and sectors in the workforce have strict criteria to follow.

Whether you have been in your profession for decades or not, it is important to have a process of some type to fall back on. Each company will do things a bit differently to get to their customer/clients out goal.

Even if you have a doctorate, having a process to read up on or to grab if you forgot something, is important.

Documentation is a key aspect to any Quality & Business system. If it isn't documented, it didn't happen. How will employees complete that documentation?

Processes don't have to be complicated, but they do need to get the employee in the right direction.

I am sure your customer/client will appreciate the effort to get them what they want, when they want it, the way they want it.

Keep it simple, but stay compliant to and within the contract, agreement or whatever you work from for your business.

Processes.

I see across social media sites discussions on processes.

Some are joking about the subject and some are not. Often, they are talking extremes.

Some want none. Some want too many.

How about meeting in the middle?

In many industries and companies, some processes are needed. If interested in ISO certification, among others, documentation is important.

I know I wouldn't want to work in a place with no processes. No matter your experience, each company does what they do differently. Word of mouth training is not usually efficient as each person will teach differently and dependent on requirements, may not always achieve repeatable success.

Having too many processes, steps and approvals will bog down work and create a negative environment.

Also having processes in place that employees do not quite follow because there are better ways to do it, creates potential issues.

Making a process behind the desk without input from those working it is not efficient or effective.

Take a sensible approach to what is needed to meet whatever requirements you have without going crazy. Work as a team on them to get a real process not a made-up piece of paper that is fantasy.

Keep it simple when possible.

A system of any kind in a business is only as good as the people who make it work.

Whether for Quality, Safety, Finance or anything a company needs to be successful, if the entire team is not actively using making it work, it will never be successful.

I have seen plenty of companies who use a third party to create their Quality and Safety systems. That is because the company didn't have someone within to write them. How do you think the implementation went?

Having a system on paper is of no value if it is not understood, used and correctly overseen to ensure its success.

Each company is different with different goals and employees, but it is the team who will succeed or fail for their client/customer. Success starts within.

Succeed.

Processes, Documents, why do we need them at work? Why does it matter?

Often folks do not want them because they will be held to them. They see them as a hinderance, an obstacle.

That is most certainly not the intent or point of them.

If it isn't documented, it didn't happen. In many companies and fields, work needs to be documented for the client/customer as a record the work was done. It is often how you get paid.

Regardless of the experience the employees may have, to be successful consistently, there needs to be process in place to follow. It's there to rely on when you need it and can save time by following it.

Each company is different on how work is handled, even in the same field. Relying on word of mouth training alone will not guarantee success. Build a system that allows employees to be set up for success, not in the dark winging it.

Processes don't have to be overly complicated but there needs to be something in place to work from.

This is even more important in highly regulated & technical sectors, like in Manufacturing, Software/App Development, when contracts are involved with a list of specific requirements to meet & more.

Use processes and documents to your favor. Don't treat it as just another 'necessary evil'.

Many companies have a Quality System to ensure they have in place what they need for their client/customer.

Depending on the size, scope and requirements, will determine the complexity of the system.

It should be designed to meet requirements and not become overburdened.

Have you ever heard something like this before:
"I do not want a complicated system. I don't need someone who sits in a room and knows nothing about my work telling me how to run it. I was successful before ISO and I will be successful after it."

There is to be a purpose behind setting up a system that will work for you, not against you, and meet the requirements you must follow.

The operational system to meet those requirements are designed by those in charge and need it, the process owners and Sr. Leaders.

Any Quality System is generally designed by a Quality Leader and Team, although often companies don't have that in place and it fall on whoever the Sr. Leadership deems. A Quality System is meant to ensure the business is successful, beginning to end of what they do. It is a business tool.

Use S.M.A.R.T. goals to meet your objectives and get your data, document what you need to be successful for your requirements & keep it as simple as feasible.

It is a living system, and improvements can be made at any time.

There are moments, especially in a time crunch, that having an imperfect process in place is better than none at all.

While the Process Owner should strive to ensure the written process precludes errors, deviations and other issues in the first round to prevent rework, there may be times where those issues can get worked in the second round review later.

Documents are living and can be modified at any time to get to where you need to be for the client/customer.

It is important that there is something for employees to work from, even for what may be considered simple processes.

No Quality System is perfect. If a company has a third-party audit for certification, there is usually even a minor issue found if a proper review is done. None of us are perfect, but what is important is that we try and learn from issues found.

No matter how long we have been in a job or business, it is important is to continue to learn. I certainly don't know everything and am always refreshing my knowledge and learning something new.

It is important whether it is a Quality system, Safety system, etc., that Leadership learns about it and understands it in order for it to be properly implemented by all employees in the business. Lean on others and learn from each other. Often ego prevents us from doing that.

I have seen many companies who do not have Quality within their business and although they skate by for a while, it catches up to them. Often the focus is on safety and simply getting the job done.

Quality Management when done right ensures efficient processes are in place to reduce errors, time, risk and more in order to meet the client/customers' requirements.

It is important that processes are written for employees to be successful for what their customer/client needs.

Over processing is simply a waste. Think Lean when you create a documented process. Does it make sense? Is it needed? Will it make work more cumbersome? Will the requirement be met keeping it as simple as possible?

A process is needed but don't tie employees' hands with it.

It perplexes me why companies allow employees from ground level to Sr. Leaders to either ignore processes or to not understand them. Some companies don't have Processes which is another issue altogether.

Processes are to be created by the subject matter experts and communicated to those who need to use it.

Often times training is not effective, and it is important to ensure that regardless of the position that questions are asked, and effectiveness is monitored.

Leaders especially should not pass the buck, so to speak, in regard to their processes if there is an issue. Accountability is important and issues should be owned and worked through to correct and prevent.

If there is a misunderstanding then it needs to be worked through and fingers not pointed. There are always improvements that can be made in what we do every day, even if small.

Working together and following processes as written or making needed improvements to existing processes will make a stronger organization which will flow down to the customer.

Also, often less can be more for processes, and not over complicated. You may not need a zillion documents to record what you do for your customer/client.

It is important that a business has in place a process for its employees to be successful. Surprisingly this is not the case in many companies.

Often experience is relied on, or word of mouth, hands on training, etc., but that does not ensure a standard that meets the customer/client requirements.

Even when a process is written, if it is not clear and/or the right people are involved, know and understand it, then it doesn't matter.

Transparency, clarity, involvement, oversight and communication are all vital elements to ensure a process works.

It is important for a business to look at integration of documents and/or systems. You may have 2 documents or systems when 1 may work. That is Lean in the workplace. Be efficient as a business. Get out of those silos. Communicate and the business will be stronger

---

As I have worked with hundreds of companies on Quality systems, what I find for most is that there are no processes and controlled forms in place. Getting further into the 21st century this continues to be a surprise, especially with the demands that many companies must ensure compliance for their customer/clients' requirements. Talking improvements, this may be the first one a company needs to have in order to be successful for their customer/client as well themselves.

Documentation is important for any system a business has. If there is no documentation, there is nothing to show you met requirements or provided a service to your Customer/Client.

Summary

While processes and documentation may feel like a burden and effort not wanted, it may be quite beneficial to the business once they are in place. In the end the work being done is for the customer/client and it needs to be done in a manner that will be successful for them. Without it, you will be shooting in the dark to achieve what is required as each person may do it differently, with a different outcome.

Make what you need for the workforce to use to the benefit of everyone and keep it as simple as possible to your requirements.

It is in your power.

Chapter 5
Preventing Problems

Within a process or system, it is important that regardless of the company and sector of work, that employees and leadership is ensuring what they are doing is meeting their customer/clients' requirements. Without this in place, you can most certainly have gaps or missing requirements that get out.

With any business system, whether Quality related or not, everyone involved should of course do their best to prevent issues from arising in the workplace that will impact the customer/client.

Next are some thoughts on the subject, in no particular order.

I see on a near daily basis a lack of taking issues seriously.

From a Quality standpoint, it is about ensuring requirements are being met, but more importantly to ensure the issue does not cause a problem again in the future.

That takes effort and time to review the issue, and get into the root cause analysis the way it should be done.

I see a clear lack of attention needed and time taken to ensure that the true root cause is found, let alone corrective and preventative actions taken.

Preventative actions is meant to put into place controls or eliminate the issue completely, but often times a Band-Aid is used. More often than not, training is the action taken.

How often have you forgotten something? How often have you been trained on something at work for a workplace requirement and get busy and forgot, or glossed over it? So, how will training prevent a problem from reoccurring?

Often, effort does not want to be used to put in place a good control or elimination. No time, or desire, or no money to fix a long term problem, when there really is if wanted.

This all takes leadership, both the functional area that is handing the problem, and Sr. Leadership to support with resources, time and action.

Action is really all that matters as words have no meaning without action to support it.

If a business is truly there for its client/customers and has a mission first mindset, effort and time will be used to ensure Quality of service is implemented in its entirety. Quality should never be a buzzword.

Without it, there will always be repeat issues, as well as issues period. It will impact the business, employees and client/customer's long term.

There have been so many recent debacles in the world that affected many people, shows a continuing need and importance for Quality checks in the workplace.

Whether it is aviation & IT as the hot button issues lately or manufacturing & services of any kind, ensuring what we are doing is correct to our client/customer requirements is vital.

As evident in the most recent situation in the news, one very small error can impact millions. Our actions in life, even if we don't quite think so, can have a profound effect on others.

We should do our best to make our impact positive.

There will be mistakes made along the way, but in business we should do our best to limit errors through automation or processes of some kind.

Quality is a vital aspect that is often overlooked or discounted.

Let us as a collective whole remove that from our mindsets.

Summary

A business should not want to get on the radar for allowing poor quality work getting out and negatively affecting their customers/clients and others. It will be very difficult to get back good reputation when that happens.

And yet, with that said, so many seem to get on the news for poor quality.

While it is important for all employees to prevent issues in the workplace, it is important to establish systems for employees to use to determine what an issue is, how to monitor processes, systems, actions and how to handle issues when they arise. This is where Quality Assurance and Control comes into play.

Chapter 6
Quality Assurance & Quality Control

Quality through monitoring activities is a fundamental piece to any Quality System in a business.

Whether through Assurance, Control or Testing, Quality monitoring activities is how a business ensures they are meeting requirements. Each company will do it a bit differently with who does it in the overall structure, and maybe how it is done and when it is done, but without it as part of a business there is a very good chance the customer/client may not quite get what they expected. This will harm the company in the long term.

Next are my thoughts on this in no particular order.

Often a Quality Audit is considered an intrusion, but it is not.

Ensuring as a business that you are meeting the requirements designed to be successful for your customer/client, an audit is simply a way to monitor that system.

In an ideal world, a business wouldn't need a quality team or even a safety team as the employees and leadership would engrain both in their daily tasks.

Monitoring compliance, identifying issues, correcting and preventing them through detailed root cause analysis and risk identification/reviews and finding ways to improve are some of what all employees can do.

We all play a part in the success of the business we are in as long as we remain a positive force for compliance and improvement.

Is Quality Control/Inspections a waste. Technically yes.

While there is no clear cut consensus as to what is all value added and non-value added wastes in Lean, value is what the client/customer will pay for.

Extra steps, extra work that is not truly needed to meet your client/customer requirements is technically non value added activities.

To remove Quality Control inspections, the process needs to be refined to remove any potential deviations. Will that happen 100% of the time? Probably not. There still needs to be a way to watch to ensure your product or service is to your client/customers' requirements. That is why the process needs to include a review of some sort and Quality in general needs to be monitored through the lifecycle by the function's leadership and employees. It isn't extra and needs to be part of daily tasks.

Mission first should never be a reason to let service/product quality slide and deteriorate. Your client/customers certainly won't appreciate it and could cost your business which will affect finances and jobs.

Summary

Companies need to understand at a fundamental, ground level, foundational level that Quality is a required and needed aspect of the business. It is there to help ensure they are achieving and improving what they are doing for who is paying for their services.

How a company established and maintains Quality will be different, in its structure and implementation, but having it in place is a first step towards ensuring the customer/client requirements will be met.

The second step is ensuring once it is in place that it is monitored in some fashion from beginning to end of whatever the company is doing, plus even long afterwards.

Whether through Quality Assurance and audits, Quality Control through verification, or testing of systems, oversight of activities ensures visibility and with that there is less likely a chance for failure that will hard the customer/client and company.

Chapter 7
Requirements Known & Met

Every company has some type of requirements to meet. It can be their customer/clients' requirements, local, state, federal requirements or a wide variety of others. These requirements are what will be part of what is monitored for compliance and should be built within any process/system/documents a company has. This way they are known in order to be followed.

Next are some thoughts on this topic, in no particular order.

If a company has contracts, whether with a client/customer or with suppliers, it is important that anyone involved in the contract understands it. Without understanding, compliance to it will be difficult.

Contracts can get complicated, but if the team involved in achieving the requirements don't work together, the company can fail and reputation is not easy to win back.

Ensuring methods are designed and implemented to be successful and then monitored and improved as necessary are the building blocks to success.

For a business to be successful, planning is a big part of it. Know what you need, your client/customer requirements, and get the right people in place to make what you put in place work and maintain it through checks and balances.

Communication is another important element to be successful and often times underutilized.

Lastly, never forget about looking for improvements. Often, we get used to the way things are when we should see it as they could be.

Ensuring Governance is in place is important to the success of any business, especially the larger companies. Without it in place you are at risk and compliance could be a problem that could cause issues with customers/clients.

Something that creeps up in our daily lives dependent on our jobs and industries is all about *mission first*. In that we forget about Quality and Safety. Both need to be engrained in what we do every day as we all want to be safe and go home in one piece as well as do what is required for our Customer/Client. It takes a strong Company Culture for both to succeed.

Let's talk Quality and Compliance. It is important that whatever requirements are in place to follow, if changes are needed, that they be communicated the right folks. If a Customer/Client needs thing changed it may need to go through a business Contracts department. Change can often lead to extra costs. Remember to communicate with the right people and get it documented.

A Total Quality Management System needs scheduled periodic reviews by leadership to ensure what was designed is working. This requires constant monitoring by Leadership in between Management Reviews to ensure all elements are met and all employees need to be engaged and understand they play a part. Quality is everyone's responsibility.

Many companies have subcontractors for labor, materials and equipment and it's important that this is a partnership.

It can happen where the subcontractor may at some point, for some reason, decide to do what they want their own way. Who is the prime? Who is responsible in the end and who pays whom?

This is often an important aspect of a business and can be a serious potential nonconformance if not handled properly.

An important part of a business that is not looked over in many cases are the suppliers of equipment, materials and labor. These third-party entities are responsible for so much that is not on leaderships minds. If a company does not ensure oversight is in place for these important suppliers, what they may end up getting may certainly not be what they wanted or expected.

It is important that any business who does have suppliers of some kind, double check where their equipment, supplies and labor come from to ensure it truly meets requirements.

Summary

While getting the job done every day is important, it is equally important to do it the right way the first time. Rework is a waste of time, resources and money. It also causes the customer/client to lose faith dependent on the work being redone and its impact.

Even if there are unfortunately no processes in place, requirements from the customer/client should be known, again dependent on the sector of work. A goal of any company should be meeting the requirements of those that pay for their service or products.

Anyone in the workplace who is not interested in following requirements, should not be there as they are a detriment to the organization. It is important that anyone working in any job do their utmost to provide the best service possible for the customer/client.

While the culture of the company may not have created the best environment for employees, causing dissatisfaction, that can be changed when there are no employees willing to work there. Forcing a change in leadership when the customer/client becomes dissatisfied is not an ideal situation, but dissatisfied customer/clients and employees is often a sign that change is needed. Will it bring about positive change? Only time will tell.

Chapter 8
Nonconformity

Accidents happen, incidents happen, people make mistakes, systems break. It is important that there is a process on how that is handled when it happens, even if you have Quality Checks and other methods in the workplace to monitor to not have nonconformities.

How will you control the nonconformance to ensure it doesn't spread? How will correct the issue, and most importantly, how will ensure it does not repeat?

A good root cause will get you there, but it takes some effort by those involved in the fix, which may just be process owners and employees working the function. If a company has a Quality team or entity, they of course should be involved and spearheading the initiative.

Next are thoughts on this important element in a company.

Quality Escape.

Those words together are not generally a good thing.

When a product or service is released that contains a deviation/defect, whether caught before it reached the end external customer or not, it is a quality escape. This has been in the news lately and can give a business a bad reputation and lost customers.

It is important that requirements/specifications are met before leaving the assembly line or point of origin. Quality reviews throughout the process by either inspectors or Subject Matter Experts (SME) of the operation will keep an eye and minimize escapes to hopefully zero.

Quality Assurance activities meanwhile ensures the process is in place and working while looking for potential improvements.

As a team, the business will be successful for their client/customer when working together with the common goal of quality.

It is often easy to criticize others for various reasons, but it is important to look inward first. Being critical of others when you may be just as guilty doesn't help anyone.

This is important in the Quality and Safety world where compliance is checked and measured. Is Quality and Safety, for example, compliant to requirements as well.

It is important to have everything in order yourself before going out and expecting others to be.

Escalation.

There are times where a situation cannot be handled and you have to elevate it to the next authority.

Whether it is in a customer service job or in Quality/Safety and issues are found, if the issue cannot be resolved through a variety of reasons then it must be passed on for resolution.

For Quality and even Safety, often when a nonconformant situation is discovered and submitted to the functional area leadership, they may either not have the ability to handle it or no interest. In this case there may be no choice but to pass it up the chain to the next authority.

If the Quality or Safety culture is strong within a company, especially starting with the Sr. Leadership, then it will be handled properly.

If not, well, the company will be at risk until the situation is resolved.

Usually better to have a lower risk level in business.

Summary

While we strive for excellence and perfection, it will not be 100% of the time, even with the best systems in place.

It takes everyone working within a company to take ownership of identifying, containing, correcting and preventing any and all nonconformances. Whether is it considered small or not, a deviation is a deviation. Once identified it can be looked at for further controls in that function, because sweeping issues under the rug will only further escalate small issues into larger ones over time.

Everyone needs to take it seriously and act timely to mitigate risk of the issue progressing further. Sitting on a problem will not make it better.

Only Sr. Leadership in a company can make it work and building within their culture the importance of self-identifying issues through Quality at the Source. Working the issue from the beginning till closure and onward through monitoring is vital. Missing one of the steps in corrective action could leave potential gaps. Far too often you will over time forget to maintain actions, which is why monitoring through effectiveness sampling is important, not just to close out the initial identified problem.

Chapter 9
Cost to Quality
Value Add - Non-Value Add

Yes, there is a cost to Quality, both good and poor Quality. A company cannot expect to have good quality service without putting time, effort and yes, finances towards it.

The goal is to have good Quality and not poor Quality as it will end up costing more. I have seen far too often a lack of Quality within companies that end up costing them contracts, reputation and employees. Many of the companies I have worked with did not have a Quality rep. They utilized Project Managers or other positions with little to no Quality experience among them, and the results showed. Often their focus was on safety and project management but ignoring the quality aspect and contractual requirements that builds both as a foundation.

Next are some thoughts on this, in no particular order.

There is a cost to conformance. It doesn't happen with hope and luck. It takes effort and should be incorporated into any budget. Trying to skimp on it will end up costing more later.

Often, and I have seen too many companies do this, Quality is not a thought. There is no one doing it.

Then something happens.

Then it becomes important after there is a loss of either money or reputation, sometimes both.

Be proactive and not reactive. Get everyone involved in Quality. Quality, no different than Safety, needs to be part of our tasks at work.

Lower your risks.

Non-Value-Added Wastes are something that can drag down any organization. Often, they won't even know what they are doing is non-value added, but there are plenty of examples to find any workplace.

Value added activities is what your customer/client wants and should be the focus. There are some business related activities needed even though they are deemed as non-value add for various reasons.

The primary focus is to remove all the unnecessary stuff we do and you'd be surprised how much time and money can be saved.

Think TIMWOOD and DOWNTIME when looking for non-value added wastes in the workplace.

When you take some time to look around, you would be surprised at the amount of wastes there may be. Could be small, yes, but it can add up. I have worked many improvement projects that started small and ended up making a big impact over time.

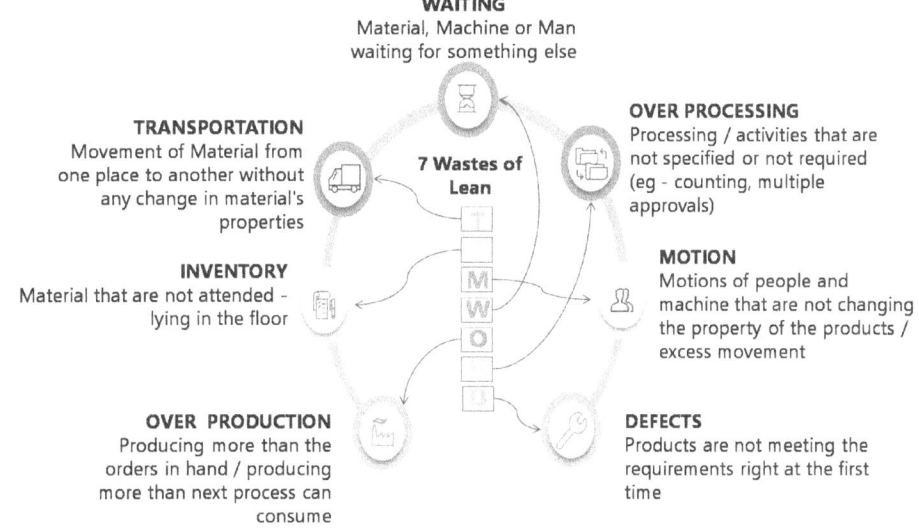

Credit (No Relationship with Company)- Picture from: https://www.csensems.com/muda/

Credit (No Relationship with Company)- Picture from: https://kissflow.com/project/agile/8-wastes-of-lean/

Summary

When you look, really look, you will often find a lot of waste in the workplace through what you thought was needed activities. They often turn out to be non-value added wastes of time and effort. Eliminating these, which may be challenging at first, will make a smoother workplace through a reduction of excess, issues and movement which the employees will come to find extremely welcoming once implemented.

You must have an open mind when it comes to looking around your area for improvements, as you often have blinders on. I have heard many times that leaders believe they are either good to go, or they don't want to rock the boat for their employees as change is not always taken in a positive light.

It is not easy, but the reason for the change needs to be broken down to show the improvement, and even then, I have seen where only after a change was made was it truly seen and appreciated.

Chapter 10
Improvements

A part of what Quality does within a company, in addition to monitoring the work against the requirements, is looking for and assisting with improvement.

Improvements are not always welcomed as, again talking from experience, leadership believes what is in place is working fine. It can take a great deal of effort to explain, show through data and get buy in with leadership to implement improvement ideas. Often, even after providing data showing there can be an improvement made, leadership doesn't want to do it because they don't want to make the effort. Yes, it takes effort to enact improvements, but that effort backed by data and proper planning, should be embraced by leadership. Improvements are to make a workplace and overall a company more efficient, which can most certainly assist their bottom line dependent on what the improvement touches on.

Next are some thoughts on this important aspect of Quality, in no particular order.

While improvements are important to look at in the workplace, it is important to know and understand that it is an improvement.

This is why a study or analysis is important to do before implementation. Don't just do an improvement for the sake of it or to make a name for yourself. Make the improvement because it will actually benefit the company and client/customer.

New leaders will often try to implement a bunch of changes, often will little to no thought or plan and it backfires.

Those who just took a process improvement course and got a six sigma belt may also jump at doing an improvement. Plan it out.

Communicating ideas and getting feedback and concurrence is important to making a process improvement stick and become a part of the Quality culture.

Is automation considered an improvement?

Of course.

Using technology in the workplace can reduce errors, simplify the work, remove manual methods, paperwork, create/maintain standards & overall make a more efficient output for the client/customer.

Automation, like any type of Improvement, needs to be done after the process is in place. Sometimes a first step of an improvement is actually creating a process to follow and then making it better.

If a business has a system in place to look for improvements, especially if there is a Quality System in place, document it.

Give credit and praise to those who are trying to make the company better internally and for the client/customer. Shouldn't matter if it is a small or big idea.

Using software to improve is just one tool/method in the innovation toolbox.

IT shouldn't be in a silo, just like all other departments. Quality, IT, Finance and others can collaborate to improve the business.

Talk is easy, ideas... depends and execution can be the tricky part.

The person who may have come up with the idea may not be the one to execute it.

It often takes a team to make something happen, but one person can make a difference in supporting it.

Brainstorming is great but it is even better to see an idea come to life.

See it through with support and get away from all the talk, and it will happen.

There are a lot of great ideas out there. Some make it and some don't. Some get leadership buy in, some don't. Persevere if you have a great idea, if it has merit. Timing also needs to be factored in as it may not always be the right time to enact.

Just don't give up on a great idea.

Process Improvements are meant to be a positive situation/scenario at work.

There are many ways to work one and document it, but small or big, an positive improvement is moving in the right direction.

While companies may prefer and focus on hard savings to help their bottom line, ignoring other elements of improvements doesn't help the culture.

You want employees involved and interested in conducting these improvement projects. Limiting them to only one way or one tool when there are many, will quickly put a damper on their enthusiasm.

To continue to drive towards efficiency to meet the customer/client requirements, leadership needs to support and promote continual process improvement in all its glory.

It is difficult at times to focus and concentrate with so much going on around us.

There may be times we just need to step away for a moment and clear our minds.

Everyone is different with different situations. One way won't work for everyone.

The solutions may not always be easy either.

A lot of great ideas aren't always the easiest to implement. Just try them in small steps and see what works.

Small steps are better no steps.

Even small steps can feel daunting at times. I don't have time or I don't feel like it today may enter your mind.

Stay focused and those small steps will become a habit.

Push through and in time it will become common place and you will look down a mountain of small steps you have taken.

Everyone's path is different. Focus on your path.

We may strive to get things the most perfect we can, but perfect is often out of reach.

Getting something done is often an accomplishment by itself as it is better than not doing anything at all.

Small steps are important and as those steps are taken, it will often get better.

There are times that we over complicate what we do.

We may not know better. Often, it's a mindset of it's always been done that way or we are doing x, y, z because we are going above and beyond for the customer.

Does your client/customer want the extra work you are doing? Is it necessary to meet requirements?

Improvements can be as simple as taking away a step not needed.

Use automation instead of a form or do you need all the forms you are using?

There are plenty of ways you can look around and make things easier on yourself, if you try.

No one wants to give up on an idea they are passionate about, but there are at times and situations where we might just have to shelve it.

At work, even with a great plan, presentation and motivation by the project lead, if the entire team or Sr. Leadership is not on board, the project may languish.

Priorities may change, other needs arise, funding dries up, or a number of other reasons.

The idea can always be taken off the shelf again, but expending time, energy and resources pushing to get it off the ground may in the end be fruitless and pointless. There are times that patience is the key to success in both work and our personal lives. Not always easy though.

Often people feel they need to make these big leaps in something, whether an improvement idea at work, their personal lives or just life in general. When you go big right out the gate, it's easier to get discouraged when it doesn't work. Small steps each day consistently will get you to your goal.

In Quality when working improvement projects, often folks want to hit it big to make a big impression. While that is great, completing small Kaizen and 5/6S projects can add up to a big impact.

Reach out for help when you need it.

Have an idea you want to present at work?

Think Elevator Speech.

The idea is to keep the speech short, generally around a minute.

What is the issue you want improved & the solution are the biggest elements of the speech.

INTRODUCTION
Briefly tell your audience who you are and what your current position is.

EXPERIENCE
Provide a one-sentence statement about your relevant experience.

GOALS
Hook the audience with a goal statement that clearly communicates what you are asking for.

SOLUTION
State your idea for achieving the goal you have identified.

PLAN
Now that you have laid out your goals and solution, be more specific about your plan.

Credit (No Relationship with Company)- Picture from: https://www.smartsheet.com/content/elevator-pitch-templates

How often do you see multiple people doing one task or one doing a task with multiple others standing around? I do.

From both a Quality and Leadership aspect, waste as well as more efficient methods to complete tasks, needs to be looked at.

It will be better for the business as well as for the customer.

This is the essence of Lean.

Small steps can add up. Don't always think you have to make huge gains and improvements in the short run. This is for your personal life and at work.

Kaizen means small, good change, so congratulate yourself for even the smallest improvement.

A business, especially a larger company, should not constrain employees on ways to identify Improvements in the workplace.

A positive Quality Culture will allow employees some freedom to use the wide variety of methods and tools out there for Lean, Six Sigma or a combination to capture how they can do things better, faster, more efficiently & smarter which will then trickle down to the customer/client which is the ultimate goal.

Leaders, to include Quality, need to keep an open mind and open doors to employees and not close doors and tie hands.

Another thought on Improvements as it should be continual but one thing to remember is requirements. As shown in the previous chapter, we should always look at Lean using the Muda (Wasteful) mindset with TIMWOOD/DOWNTIME and non-value added activities, but a customer/client may have a requirement where you need what you may think of eliminating. Always ensure requirements are looked at first before getting rid of something as you may need it.

Improvements both in our personal lives as well as work life should be continual.

In the workplace it should not be considered extra. Mission first mentality will put Quality and Safety on the backburner and that is not healthy for a business. Quality and Safety should be part of the mission and finding improvements to both will often make the mission stronger, better, easier and smarter for the business and customer/client. In the end it may make some money or save it.

I've heard it from top leadership in the past that there is no time for it and that is not good for the culture of the company. The system can be designed, setup, and implemented to document improvements but Quality and Safety cannot force anyone to do them. That takes Sr. Leadership to drive it.

Taking a little time for improvements may save much more in the long run.

There are plenty of methods and tools out there to use to document improvements, but the important thing is that we look for ways to improve what we do for our customers/clients.

Small or big, an improvement is an improvement. Within a quality system, if followed to ISO standards, improvement is continual.

Summary

It is important to remember that improvements are continual. It isn't a one-time event. It is something everyone should be looking at internally at how they can do better. It takes some time, effort, and possibly some finances to start, but long term it will save time, effort and finances when done properly.

It takes everyone to participate, top down across the company to be successful.

Whatever method or tool you use to initiate, document and complete the improvement, give yourself and others involved credit once completed. Celebrate the improvement, small or big. It takes effort to do and those involved should get congratulated.

Motivation comes in different forms. At the very least, a pat on the back and a thank you, can go a long way.

Chapter 11
Quality Culture & Buy In

Culture. An often-reviled word these days in business, but without it, certain aspects like Quality and Safety will fail.

Buy in by both leadership and the general workforce is the #1 things that is needed for any system to truly work. Without buy in, nothing matters. It doesn't matter if it is Quality, Safety, Human Resources, Finance, Supply, IT, Security. You don't get people interested in participating, it will fail.

Next are some thoughts on this, in no particular order.

You cannot force buy in.

It doesn't matter the system or requirement; you cannot force anyone to care or follow it. Yes, you can have mandatory training. Yes, you can discipline. In both cases if the individual (s) doesn't care, or isn't interested, it really will not matter the steps taken with or against them.

Culture is not easy to grow regarding Quality, Safety and other aspects. It takes time, effort, strong leadership to drive it and employees interested to be a part of it.

As much as we want everyone to be on board immediately, often there will be times that ideas & systems need to be sold to the team, especially to Sr. Leaders. We may not think it should, especially in the realm of Quality & Safety, but as it takes time, and in the end money, to build and maintain it is understandable.

Everyone though should have an open mind. You'd be surprised how certain systems, when designed and implemented correctly, can benefit and help you.

The company culture will define how the company operates for the employees within and how the client/customer will be treated.

Culture is important.

The culture should attract the right people, remove the wrong people, treat everyone well and equal and be a positive environment to succeed for all clients/customers.

It takes the Sr. Leaders to establish and foster the positive culture and drive downward to all employees to be a part of it.

If not, the Quality of the work will not be optimal, Safety will not be important and the overall business functions will deteriorate.

Quality will often get a bad rap for being the "police" who go around looking for problems. That may be the case sometimes but should not be the intent.

If done properly, Quality is infused within an operation. A dedicated Quality Team may not be needed if all employees employ it within their operation from beginning till end.

I know I did when I worked in the operation side of the house, before moving to Quality full time. I assessed myself and the workplace daily against requirements. I incorporated continual improvements in the operation. I updated processes when needed to catch something new, no longer needed or just lean it.

When Quality finds something not quite right in the operation and reports it, and it is captured within a non-compliant report and issuance of a corrective action to the function, they are treated with distain or at least indifference. A pariah even.

It is on the function, all employees, to include leadership, to identify issues in their area and work to contain, correct and prevent reoccurrence. This means not fixing without documenting a root cause and subsequent actions and especially sweeping under the rug, hiding/ignoring it which is the worst.

You should never wait for it to become a real problem that will affect the client/customer. You should never wait for Quality to find it. Implement Quality at the Source.

Know (everyone) your operation, understand it, monitor it and report on it.

Summary

While some company cultures are either fake, nonexistent, or toxic, for Quality, Safety and other aspects within the company, a culture where all employees play a part is needed for success. Getting everyone on board is essential for these types of aspects in a business because without the people involved, failure is imminent.

Any company that is serious about treating their employees with respect will ensure a culture is promoted for the betterment of the employees and company as a whole. People that have a voice, their opinions heard, where improvements and innovation is welcome, is where a company will thrive for their customer/client.

If not, don't be surprised when the company dies on the vine.

Chapter 12
Keys to Working Quality

I have often been asked what is needed to work in Quality as a profession. It isn't always an easy answer. Quality has many different facets within it across services, manufacturing, medical, IT and more, so the requirements differ slightly for each. Additionally, each company and leadership expect different requirements to meet from experience, education and certification.

While some of these are important, I have found some of the best auditors had no experience or certifications when they started. It is important to use good judgement when selecting someone for an auditor role.

Next are my thoughts on this topic, in no particular order, and some may repeat.

Working Quality is not easy.

It takes a special kind of special to fill the role.

You are usually ostracized, which is unfortunate.

Not everyone has the personality, the skills, the ability to perform the job at a high level.

You need excellent reading, writing and verbal experience. You cannot be effective if you cannot clearly speak to an auditee or other auditors. Writing clear, legible reports is an important part of any auditors' tasks. Reading through various requirements is an important part to planning as an auditor.

Auditors need to be flexible throughout the day as you may need to adjust your tasks to move to a hot topic. There will be times this will be frustrating as it can make a challenging situation and list of tasks even more difficult, but you need to push through.

Organization is key to success because as an auditor you may have to juggle multiple tasks, and auditees. You need to be able to organize and schedule everything on your plate in a timely manner. Multi-tasking, although not usually truly effective or efficient, may become a part of life.
Part of this is planning, which is another important skill that you will need to use daily.

Ability to utilize automated systems, as well as review some old school paperwork.

Remember to trust but verify what is said and given to you. Some may feel Quality is the police, laying down the law, but that is not true. Quality though often provides a bit of detective work through auditing and assisting with root cause analysis. You need to be able to look at the granular, the fine detail that others may or will not. Critical thinking, analytical thinking will allow you to find both issues and improvement opportunities that the functional area may overlook, as well as help correct and improve the findings.

Independent capability & teamwork will be needed as both may be required dependent on the task, the auditee and business.

Honesty & integrity are key aspects all those involved in Quality, and is really a must.

In the end be resilient and adapt to your environment as an auditor as the environment may change often if you travel.

To track governance, risk, and controls in a workplace, there will usually be an auditor in place or at least someone who does the task.

This position requires certain aspects the individual needs to have in order to be successful.

Some and not all, and not in any order:

Integrity.

Honesty.

Must be an Effective Communicator.

Good at Building Relationships.

Be good with Tech. A Quality System may be digital in nature.

Be willing to learn.

Be open to innovative.

Be detail oriented.

Be Approachable.

Collaborative.

Strategic.

Problem Solver.

Excels with Time Management.

and more...

Quality take a wide ranging skill set.

Whether it is:

- Quality Assurance where you are monitoring compliance through a risk based schedule using process, system or product audits, or assisting process owners with improvements;

- Quality Control where you are inspecting and monitoring daily activities for compliance;

- or Quality Testing in the IT field;

Each of these takes skills to learn and master.

While it is important to be knowledgeable in the Quality world, it is also important to understand what you are auditing. That takes effort and time to research and gain knowledgeable on.

Soft skills and hard skills are needed in this profession. Not everyone can be an auditor, just like not everyone can be a leader.

That may take trial and error to find out. Don't be discouraged immediately if you find it difficult.

Building relationships is a key part to be a Quality Professional. That might be hard for some, especially introverts.

Quality can be lonely, as in many companies the department is often ostracized as the operations rarely enjoy feedback through audits, or audits themselves turn them off.

Audits are an opportunity to improve and grow in addition to ensuring requirements are being met. That sounds nice, but people don't always want to improve and grow, and to change what they are used to.

Long term, companies need to come together and work together as one unit and not as separate silos of functions. ignoring each other and not supporting each other will cause a cancer to grow.

Don't be the start of that cancer.

When Quality Professionals are used for things that are not Quality related, it #1 is a waste of talent and #2 it leaves the company at risk. It takes their time and focus away from ensuring compliance is met as well as working improvements and other Quality related tasks.

Some companies have Quality included with Safety, Environmental, and Health related functions. While I include a lot of Safety related topics together with Quality because of their similarities, the jobs are quite different with different requirement.

Often companies don't have Quality and rely on PM's, Ops, an engineer or some other role to most likely save money because they don't feel the cost of Quality is worth it. I have seen that backfire many times.

If you do have a specific Quality Professional and you are using them to hunt down unrelated information to Quality or going around doing odd ball things, again unrelated to Quality, you are wasting their talent and ability and probably shouldn't have them to begin with.

Leadership in any company, especially the larger size, needs to take Quality serious for their customer who normally expects Quality products and services.

That takes effort, time and yes, money. If not invested in Quality and Safety, among other functions, the Cost of Poor Quality will put you in a reactive and dangerous position long term.

It is disappointing when Quality Professionals return to the operations side and either forget their Quality knowledge and don't use it in their daily activities, or they become anti-Quality which is terrible.

I was the opposite when I was on the operations side of the house. I did 30+ internal documented assessments a month on my requirements, worked process improvements and identified when things went south, which was rare as I kept a close eye on the workplace.

I got my Six Sigma/Lean Six Sigma Green and Black Belt from working process improvements in the operation before I went into Quality full time. Often folks will simply get a certificate and not actually use the principles they learned from getting the piece of paper. It won't matter unless you use it.

For the last year and a half I have tried to convey short, simple messages across a number of platforms on the message of Quality, best business practices, improving leadership skills & in all that... communication.

There is a small group here on this platform that speak on Quality and its importance. It often feels as though we are spinning our wheels. But regardless of the audience size, if even a small group hear the message and it resonates, and they take the message to others then it is successful. Even if it feels small at times.

Leadership in any organization is the driving force behind either advancing or moving the company backwards. Leadership needs to take time and effort and learn a bit about Quality, Safety and the many elements that make a company successful. They don't have to be experts. That is why they hire the experts. They just need to understand why they are all important. Why it matters in the end to have a successful, well rounded business. Why they and all the employees should care.

It takes effort, interest and time.

Not doing so will quite possibly in the long run cost even more effort and time to go back and fix.
Dealing with issues that wouldn't have been a problem if handled correctly at the correct time, if everyone engrained these ideas into their daily mindset at work, would save a lot of heartache for a lot of people around the world.

It is important that while Quality Professionals assist, mentor, educate and overall support the operations of a business, that they not become a crutch.

Too often the operations will rely on Quality instead of taking ownership themselves. In turn when something negative occurs, Quality is blamed instead of the operational leaders.

Remember that at the end of the day it is the operations processes and systems to build, maintain and monitor. Assisting is not owning the process or system. As with anything in life, responsibility and accountability are hallmarks of what makes a company and team great.

The situation should be mutually beneficial, not one sided. Quality should not be leaderships... lackey, for a better word. Generally speaking, they should not be the ones doing the random odd ball tasks, random errands for leadership, non-Quality related jobs that take their focus away from compliance and improvements. There are of course times in a company there are other duties assigned to meet internal needs, but they should not be abused.

If a Quality Professional is hired into a Quality related role, same for Safety, HR, Finance, etc., that needs to be their focus, with Sr. Leaderships understanding. If not, what is the point?

Often someone will be tasked with providing Quality oversight or assistance that is a secondary job. Same could be for Safety, Health or Environmental oversight. Time needs to be taken and given by leadership in order to do it successfully. It is a benefit for the company, not hinderance to spend time on these important tasks that should already be a part of the fabric of a company.

Just like the phrase, 'It's always been done that way,' saying 'mission first' as a reason to bypass requirements will have a high likelihood of making the client/customer unhappy if it isn't to specs because certain aspects were glossed over.

For those in the Quality business, it can be lonely. For many in the business world, Quality isn't liked because it is felt they are telling subject matter experts and leadership what to do and more importantly what they are doing wrong.

This is a false ideal. Quality personnel, when doing things properly, are simply to ensure compliance against the client/customer requirements are being met as well as looking for way to improve the workplace with leadership.

In a perfect world, every business would have Quality incorporated into what they do and staying compliant would be second nature.

This isn't a perfect world.

Quality personnel are there to help not hinder.

When Quality was there to audit my department, it honestly felt like an annoyance because between External and Internal audits, there was upward to a dozen audits a month which was time consuming.

As much as feasible, Quality should not hinder the operation to ensure compliance is being met. Not always easy, but should be a goal.

Together, Quality and the Operations in a company need to work hand to hand to ensure they are providing their client/customer the best service/product possible.

How does one become a Quality Professional?

Good question.

While you can go to certain colleges and major in it, once out you need to find an entry level job and many companies expect some experience.

You may be looking for a new career, but have no direct experience.

Both are the typical catch 22 that many find themselves in.

Now as for my experience, I did a little Quality Control in my teens while working retail. After that period, I didn't really think of Quality for around 12 years.

In my previous career I began to learn about the various aspects of Quality and engrained it into my workplace as I was in charge. I took ISO 9001:2008, and eventually worked my way up to Six Sigma Black Belt, on my own time and dime. I used that knowledge to make improvements in the workplace.

When I decided to shift to a new career in Quality, I had that in my utility belt, so to speak. It was possibly easier to get a job in Quality having it, but each company handles hiring and requirements differently. I would recommend if you are interested in Quality, learn about it. Once you learn about it, use it. It isn't of any value if you don't use and demonstrate it.

Not everyone is cut out for Quality. I have hired folks with zero Quality background that turned out to be the best hires and Quality Auditors. I have also seen some that just wasn't capable of doing it.

To be truly successful you can't just be a checklist auditor. You must have a bit of an investigative mindset but also understand how to interact and communicate with people in order for the process to be successful.

Quality are not cops and should never be out to get anyone. That will cause the process to fail and the relationships to break.

The goals should be to ensure everything in a business is running as it should, meeting the client/customer requirements. Secondly, looking for processes to lean. Quality is there to help improve the workplace to make the company better for the future and its bottom line and simply making more efficient processes for employees to use in their daily tasks.

Quality should always be perceived as a positive addition, a value add to everyone and not a negative.

Don't let not getting some jobs get you down as it may take some time to get a foot in the door. Keep trying if it is what you want.

Quality Professionals often come from a wide variety of fields.

There are Quality degrees you can get when young and starting off, but Quality may be a second or third career for some.

Bringing in that expertise from another career only enhances your time in Quality.

Quality has so many types of fields to work in, it may surprise folks.

Manufacturing, Retail/Services, Medical (which has a lot by itself), Food, Technology (IT), Logistics and more.

There is so much to learn within the Quality field for a lifetime. And what is important is that Quality becomes a regular facet in those fields. Quality and Safety are integral parts in what we do every day for the client/customer. It is often not even thought about, but it is important.

Often Quality gets a bad rap for over complicating processes and what is done within a company.

Let's just get the mission done, customer first, everything else isn't important.

Well the point is to ensure that what is being done for the client/customer is correct. That is why Quality is important.

When a nonconformance is found, especially from a third party or the client/customer, the function affected tends to go overboard with corrections.

It isn't Quality in this case that is over complicating matters. Keep the corrections and preventative actions simple, yet enough to tackle the problem.

Don't automatically go to a person is at fault. It can certainly be the process or something else. People do make mistakes though and that is why when possible it is important to automate the process to remove the potential errors.

Corrections and preventative actions aren't always easy to come up with. That is where brainstorming through the root cause analysis and conducting a Gemba can help.

One person may not have all the answers.

Don't judge Quality without also looking within.

A Career.

Some may want one, some may not. Some may have multiple careers in their lifetime, some may have one.

If you want a career, that path is yours to take from ground level to the top as far as you can go in a business. It may take many years to get the knowledge and expertise to climb to the top of the ladder.

It generally takes many thousands of work hours over years to become an expert in a job/field.

Along the way, leadership should be supporting the growth of employees, not holding them back. A business will benefit from experienced employees who can continue to contribute and improve how the business runs.

No leader should either hold an employee back or expect them to move down or laterally in the company unless there are contributing factors at play due to performance or other outlier.

Companies will just hemorrhage good employees with that mindset and hurt themselves in the long run.

In the Quality world, even Safety & Environmental, people get degrees in these fields. Most don't think of that when they think those type of jobs. While many moves into the jobs from outside and learn about what is needed, these can certainly be careers for many.

Companies can leverage the experience over time to continue to make the company more profitable through reduction in waste & deficiencies, stay in line with client/customer requirements and keep them satisfied, reduce risk & educate, mentor & assist the workforce to work Quality & Safety into their work.

While Quality is not the police, they do tend to put on the investigator cap when needed to root out issues to prevent recurrence or bigger issues from occurring.

Regardless of the industry, this is an important part of a good Quality system and an important trait needed in a Quality Professional. This needs to be kept in mind because not everyone has the interest in digging into matters to help find those issues. If you just want to read off a checklist, it may not be the right fit for you.

Summary

How each person gets into Quality as a profession will be different. Some may not need experience and learn as they go along. Some companies may want a list of experience, certificates and knowledge to start, some may not.

There are a lot of facets within Quality across the many fields out there, whether, services, manufacturing, medical, financial or IT.

There is a lot to learn in Quality, especially if you are covering multiple functions within a company.

If you are interested in Quality, learn about it first. Use it in your current role to test it out and your capabilities. You may not like it when you go to use it in your workplace. You may love it and decide that is what you want to transition to.

It may take time to transition, but don't lose faith. It you are meant for it, you will find it.

Chapter 13
Explaining Quality

Have you had difficulty in explaining what Quality is, why it matters and its importance for a business? You wouldn't be the only one.

Although the topic should be one that leaders and employees deploy in their daily work, the topic is often not on people's minds. Few will go out of their way to learn the various aspects of Quality, even if a company has internal training on it. You must have a passion or desire to learn about it. Even if there is time after the main job gets done at work, and personal time is available, there is a litany of other things to do in the day.

Next is a thought on this subject.

Is the topic of Quality boring?

Well any topic can be boring to someone out there. It isn't always the presenter that causes a topic to be boring.

If the audience isn't interested in a topic, they simply won't show or be disengaged if there.

In companies, training is often mandatory. Training is important, but if they don't want to be there then it is difficult to get through to them. That is for leadership to handle. Leadership is the driving force to establish and improve the Quality culture in a company, which is why I often focus topics on leadership.

Talking the various aspects of a Quality System may not be engaging to some, but Quality is a vital component to any business that wants to be successful. Same can be said about Safety, Environmental, Security, Finance, HR, IT and more.

Breaking it up in small bites that can be digested in simple ways can help. That is why I have created over 400 short videos, found on a multitude of social media sites, on the many aspects of Quality in ways that I certainly hope are easier to understand to the layman.

Dependent on the social media site, there are thousands, tens of thousands to hundreds of thousands of people following along as I post them.

The goal is to spread the word of Quality and its importance across the world. Engagement is important and passing along knowledge to others who can help make Quality important in our lives is key.

Always looking for constructive opinions, thoughts, ideas from others in the Quality world because it is a diverse job sector across the world.

Summary

Communicating Quality, as with any subject takes effort, time to learn and the ability to get the subject across to the audience. Not everyone can do that, but it is important that it can be and is communicated to the masses in a manner best understood by anyone and everyone. That may require some tailoring.

I have done my best to communicate the many aspects of Quality in both the business world and social media in a manner that can be understood, which isn't always easy.

It takes a team effort across the Quality World to help educate, train and mentor anyone in leadership and anyone involved with and interested in learning about the subject.

Together we can succeed in making this important subject better known and understood for so many people around the world that are involved in providing quality services and products for so many millions and billions of people.

Part 2
Business

Chapter 1
Responsibility

Leadership in any company, in any type of business, has a responsibility to the people within, its customers/clients and anyone who has an interest in the business. Responsibility is not something to take lightly, and for someone in a leadership role, it is imperative that it is used correctly.

You will find many in a role over others who do not care for those in their charge. That is dangerous, and counterproductive.

Next are thoughts on responsibility, in no particular order.

As we move into higher positions in life we take on new and different responsibilities.

While we may have been an expert in something, we tend to change our focus to monitoring and guiding others who are doing the tasks.

Often people think that bosses and leaders should know or be able to do every task their people are doing. Maybe to a certain degree but others are in that role who are doing the daily activity.

The nuances and little steps and actions that go into any given job may not be on the boss or leaders mind as they are looking at the bigger picture.

They may be able to explain the larger steps, actions & outcomes, but they shouldn't generally be expected to know what you are doing to the smallest degree.

That is most certainly the case with multiple teams of people doing many different actions and activities each day.

When you get into a leadership role your focus and vision changes. You generally are no longer doing what you did and now must ensure others are.

Don't be a jerk to those around you, in any setting.

Many people work to live, while some live to work. In both cases we are at work, dealing with situations daily from internal and external sources.

In our personal lives we also deal with a wide variety of folks, from family to friends and strangers.

How we interact with each other can play an important part in our lives, mentally, physically and emotionally.

There should be no reason to be difficult on purpose with others. If you are, what is the root cause? We each live different lives, have had different environments, with different situations that have impacted us. These all play a part in who we are.

We all change over time.

Being difficult with each other only makes life more difficult, for all parties. If that is the intention of the one imparting the difficulties on others, I pity you and hope that there is a positive transforming event that changes your perspective on life and with others.

We all make mistakes, from leadership to employees at work, to those in our personal lives. It is important to work on those and not allow them to beat us down. Both sides need to work on it with each other.

Open communication, positive communication are needed and required for relationships to be successful in life. When people cooperate, life in both business and personal lives is easier and more successful.

Vision, goals, actions needing to be met will always work with people who are in line with them and willing to work with each other on them.

Failures in relationships occur when that cooperation and communication ends. It can be difficult and sometimes painful, but nothing in life worthwhile is easy.

Think on this next time you are sending an email or verbally chastising someone on something small, or some other minor issue. Big issues will occur from time to time of course, but let's not allow the outliers to control our view of life.

As a leader, remember that you are in your position to help those under your charge, not beat them down. Mentoring and growing your teams should be your main goal which will meet your company's goal for the client/customer.

While not all leaders are going to do and possibly understand every aspect of what their employees are doing, it is of course beneficial to be able to.

The issue really is when the leader doesn't understand the amount of work that goes into any given task.

They underestimate the work and ignore the ones doing it when they bring up issues or constraints.

It is important to listen to your team.

Also when a leader doesn't understand the work being done, they are not able to give clear answers and guidance. Part of the role of leadership is to support the team.

Knowing and understanding is a part of that, otherwise you are blind to your surroundings. In addition, dare I say, you are ignorant to your teams' plight.

Summary

Not everyone wants responsibility in life. For leadership, there is a lot of responsibility that goes along with it, and even if you are not in leadership there is still elements within your job you will be responsible for.

It is important to understand before you go into something, before you decide, that you understand the responsibility you will inherit from your decision.

In business, not everyone can handle leadership. From outside many believe they can do it, that it is easy. Once inside that circle and in that role, the situation changes.

Life will give us many decisions to make, which we need to take seriously to ensure we go down the responsible path.

Use your responsibility to better those in your charge.

Chapter 2
Leadership

Leadership is a critical role in any company, and even outside.

Next are my many thoughts on this critical subject, as leadership is not relegated to the business world alone, but all aspects of our lives.

It starts when we are young at home and in school, when we enter the working world, and even in our personal time and hobbies. Taking charge at a moment notice, making a decision that will impact friends, family, colleagues will happen. It is important to understand the many facets of this subject, to learn from great leaders around us and mentor others as we get into that role.

Leadership isn't easy. It is easy to deride leaders, to talk trash about them. Until you are in a leadership role, you truly will not understand what all is involved.

Often things look easy from the outside. It changes once it is you in the role.

There is plenty out there on training to become a leader. Things to do, to not do. I would hope no one intentionally goes out of their way to become a bad manager, supervisor or leader of people. As I have said in other posts, regardless of what some might think, not everyone is cut out for the role.

With that said I believe most of us have faced or continue to face such difficult people.

One type to avoid becoming is what is known as a seagull manager. They swoop in at a hint of issues arising, ready to crap on everyone's day. They tend to run in, complain while not really understanding the issue at hand, and then leave. They give no real solutions to the supposed problem, leaving everyone even more confused.

While they are there, they control the narrative, leaving no room for discussion. It is an title, position and ego situation at that point.

While not a guarantee to work, being assertive in the situation may break the seagull manager from continuing to crap on the room they are in.

As with all things, communication is key.

Often we are faced with either a micromanager or a seagull manager, neither of which is needed in order to have a successful team and company.

There are certain traits and goals that a good leader will possess and strive for, with bad leaders/bosses on the other end of the spectrum.

Having a clear vision for the company and employees on your team is one.

Clear, understandable and two way communication is another.

Supporting the team and giving them the ability to make decisions will grow the teams capability.

Having integrity and being accountable to one's self should be a fundamental aspect to the character of any good to great leader.

And understanding their team through emotional intelligence is critical to a well-built team with trust and empathy all around.

This isn't the old days of the business world, or at least it shouldn't be. By that I mean you shouldn't have to tough things out and put up with a negative, toxic environment driven by workaholics who put the business and unimportant tasks over living a life.

There should be no more badge of honors for putting in free hours, missing family events, getting berated and generally tolerating idiocy.

Let's get past that and work on a healthy balance in our lives. Be a good to great boss, not the opposite that no one wants to be around.

For all employees, you don't have to be a leader to have all these positive traits. You also make a place pleasant or not.

As leaders, we should not throw people to the wolves, especially new hires. That is one excellent way to keep high turnover, which costs more and causes a workplace to suffer.

New employees should be given time to adjust, trained on all internal requirements and tasks, and given the leadership's attention when questions are asked.

They should not be thrown into a workplace with no resources, no training and no assistance. That is improper leadership and management of employees.

Existing personal should also not be treated the same if something new comes up.

It is important that leadership understands it is their duty and requirement to give their employees what they need to succeed. This isn't just for the customer/client, but for themselves as a company.

If the employees don't have what is needed, the customer/client won't get what they need, and in turn the business will falter and eventually fail.

Authoritarian.

There are many types of leaders.

There are times where a mix of types is needed for different situations, such as when a leader had to make a decision that goes against the grain or has no input from others.

With that said, I have seen far too many times decisions made from leaders who never work the decision, putting undo stress on their team. It is easy to make a decision and then not do any of the work and think it is easy.

I have also seen far too many times where leaders decide on something against their teams input, which undermines and damages them.

The team you surround yourself with has knowledge, experience, opinions, ideas that should be valued and utilized. If not, the leader is a one person show and should do all the work from their decisions.

For both good and bad, decisions are to be accounted for in the end.

Let's talk about leadership who either can't make a decision and gets wishy washy when figuring out how to decide.

Part of a leader's job is to make a decision. Some are easier than others, but there are decisions to be made daily.

If a leader can't decide on something, maybe they aren't in the right line of work. If a leader keeps changing their mind, again, they may not be in the right line of work.

Situations change in the workplace, and in life in general. Change is a part of life. I believe we all know that.
A leader, though who can't decide to begin with, stick to a decision previously made or is constantly changing their mind only invites chaos. This will lead to a confused team and company and an unhealthy environment.

Another situation is a leader will not decide due to an insidious plan to undermine their people. It could be because they do not like a person or people on their team. That is not what a leader does to their team. That mindset is not for anyone in a sr. position. A leader is there to support and mentor. They grow more leaders, not kick people down.

They also empower their team to make decisions, so every idea or directive does not need to come from one sole person... them.

Don't paralyze your team. Don't paralyze the company with either on purpose lack of decision making as an attack or as a side effect of not being capable of the role of deciding.

Throughout our lives we may work for many companies.

We may change careers, look for new opportunities, look for promotions, look for money or other benefits or just want new challenges. Could be any number of reasons. It is important with that, that employees, management, leaders, not take offense with the situation.
No one should take it personal.

Whether leadership has mentored an employee, promoted them, or guided them through a career, it does not mean they should be offended when they leave for whatever the reason.

Leadership makes or breaks a business. They are the ones who drive the culture and drive expectations to meet the client/customer requirements.

If a company, and in turn the sr. leaders, are serious about quality, safety, finance, security, IT, human resources and more, they will drive to ensure they all are established and meet the need.

Actions speak louder than words as often there is a lot of talk in business but no actionable change or improvement made.

Balance is often needed to ensure internal business needs are met for all business functions but that outcomes meet the client/customer expectations.

Too often there is an imbalance in the workplace and something pays the price, such as quality or safety to meet financial goals. That will not work in the long run as there are many real-world examples to be found on the subject.

Putting people first will drive the company towards success for its clients/customers and get more business in the long term.

Ethics, transparency, openness between leaders and the rest of the company employees will keep a cohesive team who is willing to work with each other for the success of themselves and those they provide products or services for.

The consumers are no longer blind to the businesses that are putting massive profits first, leaving the employees making those profits to the gutter. This leaves a company vulnerable long term, even if the idea is to make it financially stronger. Who can trust a company that does that to employees?

There are better ways.

Law of the Lid. A concept from John Maxwell.

One of his 21 laws of leadership, the law of lid essentially shows that there is often a cap on the ability of someone to lead simply based on their ability.

Companies can be limited if their leadership has reached their ability. It may be important to bring in someone new that can complement leaders currently in place.

Leaders will often not want to admit they have reached their peak, their max knowledge and ability in a role. It is important that they acknowledge they need higher level of leadership in order to be successful. That make take further mentoring or training to break out of the Peter Principal they may be stuck in. This could maybe entail a new set of skills is needed.

Find a way to raise your lid.

Legendary Chinese philosopher Lao Tzu touches on how leadership should be through his 81 poems/verses which are still true and relevant today as they were 2,500 years ago. I suggest anyone interested in understand leadership read them.

A leader is one who sets the example for others to follow, rather than relying on their position of power to command obedience.

They are humble, flexible, patient, disciplined, and understands limitations while also keeping things simple.

Embrace creativity and build relationships.

Pass on knowledge.

You don't need to be the loudest in the room to lead.

It isn't easy to be in a leadership role. Not everyone wants it and not everyone is cut out for it.

Do not make it harder through self-sabotage.

What are some conditions considered to be self-sabotage you may say?

Here are some. Have you seen any of these in your daily lives?

- Not asking for other people's opinions or expertise, when a leader probably has plenty on the team to lean on.

- Reprimanding/punishing the team for any expression of disagreement. Employees should be able to offer dissenting opinion if/when warranted.

- Taking credit for other people's work & not giving praise when it's due. Certainly not passing along the leaders' failure to the team.

- Leaders acting as though they are more important than their team. Ego sometimes gets to be a bit big in a higher position. We need to remember we all started somewhere.

- Questioning other people's decisions and knowledge, especially for more seasoned team members.

- Belittling the teams' skills or accomplishments. We all may have different abilities to contribute to the team.

- Making important changes without telling anyone sets a bad example and dependent on the change can be potentially devastating.

- Finding mistakes in everything the team does. We all make mistakes and we are all not perfect. Nitpicking excessively will just contribute to poor morale. There are better ways to go about looking to improve outcomes of products/services the team may provide.

- Putting the needs of the leader ahead of the team is not healthy. A leader should be there for the team, to support them.

- Do not undermine yourself by undermining your team as a leader, thinking it will benefit you in any way.

It is important that leaders listen, really listen, to their team. Often when you get into a certain level position you are expected to know everything, have the answers, be the go to person.

A team though is usually made up of experienced people to rely on, and that includes leadership.

If leadership will not listen and uses a my way or the highway mindset, they soon will not have a team. No one will be interested in giving ideas and certainty not want to be involved or in a place when their opinions do not matter.

People cannot grow and expand their abilities if they are not allowed to try something different. Shutting down ideas and thoughts at work is simply detrimental long term.

Teams are made up of all types of experiences and it's up to those in leadership and those with the experience to train, mentor and help grow less experienced employees to become the future masters of their art.

It is important to listen, especially for a leader.

Too many times leaders will go with their thought process without listening to their team. They may approach their team to get an opinion, having already made up their mind.

It is important to get ideas and thoughts from your team because they may have something that didn't cross your mind.

It is also respectful to the team which will be reciprocated.

If not you will have a team who will be unwilling to give feedback and your team, and in turn, business will suffer.

You may not always agree with the thoughts and ideas, but they were heard.

You also may be surprised with what your team has to offer.

You will often hear that people are born leaders, but that isn't entirely true.

While some may be naturally charismatic, which helps them as leaders, it often takes a lot of work and effort to become a leader. It is a lifelong pursuit.

Experience is a big factor as you are continually learning as you go through life.

Don't be afraid to ask questions and learn from those around you. Take classes and trainings when you can. Absorb knowledge.

Never stop learning and don't be afraid to make mistakes. We should learn from them and improve. Remember that when others do the same.

Mentor the next generation of leaders when the time comes.

Often times when a new leader takes over a team, they jump straight in and start making decisions and changes.

While this may occasionally be needed in some cases, the majority of the time it is important to take some time first.

Get to know the team, what they do, why they do it before making changes.

What they are doing may be working or they could use some improvement.

Especially for new leaders, you will not know everything. It is okay to learn from those around you as you grow into the role.

Those who have been in leadership for a long time, you can still learn from those around them, and what may have worked for them in the past may not work in another leadership role.

Remember to listen and not just talk. Learn your teams' capabilities and delegate when needed. Empower the team.

Keep communication channels open.

Establish trust because without it, it is all for naught.

As you are establishing yourself, goals need to be clearly outlined for employees to meet for the success of the team. Be open and honest.

First 30 to 90 days in a new leadership role is important to show everyone what you have what it takes.

Yes, there is a difference between a Manager and Leader.

Managing is ensuring the workplace is running smoothly to meet the mission. Following a set process to meet requirements, looking for efficiencies and solving issues through controls.

A leader looks to motivate, to encourage the workforce through a vision to achieve. Giving clear guidelines and goals to follow, mentoring and pushing employees to succeed in a positive manner.

They look around to see what can be changed for the better to move the team and company into the future.

Not everyone can be a successful supervisor or manager and not everyone can be a successful leader. Not all managers are leaders.

Leaders are not born; they are made through life experiences. Leaders are those who people want to follow, not because they have to due to authority, but because they want to.

Titles are temporary.

Be a leader who takes accountability, not throwing their team under the bus when issues arise.

Be a leader people want around.

Be a leader with or without a title.

Leadership is a driving force at work. It can be a driving force for good or bad.

Everyone has bad days, but if leadership is consistently negative, it will drive good employees away and affect the client/customer relationship.

Communication is a consistent issue across many organizations.

Leadership is supposed to be there for employees, to help, mentor and guide them. Passing blame to them, setting unrealistic expectations and nitpicking their mistakes and weaknesses will not improve a thing.

The workplace should be intimidation free and open and clear with intent and goals.

Without that you will have chaos and inefficiencies.

Putting in place the right people and letting them do their job and be creative will build trust and will improve morale which spills over to the client/customers.

Not treating the workforce with dignity will in a short time create a unsafe, low quality environment that will affect the business.

That is bad for business.

It is a sad day when leadership would ever purposefully create a negative workplace by managing employees out. No one should ever want that.

The backbone of a company are the employees who work each day to achieve the requirements set forth by the client/customer.

While some employees may not be at peak performance, it is leaderships role to mentor them and get them to where they are productive.
That may not happen at the end of the day but managing out is also used on employees who are not having performance issues.

That is where ethics get fuzzy.

The question is, why go that route?

Rarely is micromanager and absentee manager a good thing and combined it certainly isn't.

It is generally the goal to be a balanced manager.

It's important to be there for your team, supporting them in their daily activities.

Encouraging and mentoring the team is what leadership is meant to do as the team's success is a plus for everyone involved.

Not being there for team meetings, cancelling meetings, not responding to emails or messages, not providing positive feedback are all negative indicators.

It is important that leadership knows their team and interacts with them in a positive manner. Not overbearing and certainly not in quick bursts that stress out the team.

Balanced is key.

Whether it wants to be heard or not, not everyone is capable of being in a leadership role and be successful at it.

As a leader it is important to not let the position go to one's head. A leader is there to support the team who supports the customer. If that support is not there, there will be no team and eventually no customers.

We are all human and should be treated as such, not numbers or disposable... unless there are aliens among us. ;)

There may be times that you are either in a leadership role but with no real authority or you are not in a leadership role but need to get a task done with a team with no clear leader.

Either case is not ideal, nor easy.

Every company will have its own type of organizational structure. Some positions may be temporary as well.

You will need to do the best in the situation.

Building relationships with the team is important. Networking may very well assist in getting goals met.

Communicating roles and goals will keep everyone on track. Don't be shy to ask questions and check in on progress. Use your expertise but remember others may know something you don't.

Earn their trust and respect.

Everyone has some level of responsibility in their position, regardless of title.

While it is important for everyone to keep learning as they get older, even leadership, it is also important that leadership mentors those around them.

Learning and mentoring takes initiative and work and will only be successful with those interested from both sides.

As we learn it is important to pass along that knowledge and not keep it bottled up.

Be involved in those around you.

It is important, whether at work or in our personal lives, to walk the walk and talk the talk.

Too often there are some who tells one thing but does another. What makes it worse is when they hold others to it but won't do it themselves.

In a leadership role that is rarely looked upon favorably.

From a Quality perspective, it is important that once a system is designed and setup, that everyone work together as a team and walks the walk towards compliance to their client/customer requirements.

It is important that employees are given an opportunity to voice opinions, concerns, ideas openly.

When their voices are ignored or shut down, the business will suffer. Having a single point of view or only Sr. Leaderships opinion leaves potential for many gaps to occur in how work is done for the customer.

You will also lose your best and brightest who will not want to waste their time in a place where their talents are not being used.
Burnout can also contribute to the situation.

Taking care of employees, and getting and using their opinion/ideas will in the long term take care of the customer.

There are a number of styles leaders can lead by.

Some may be better used in certain circumstances than others.

While I feel a hybrid of democratic and servant leader may be best in most ideal situations, there may be times that quick calls and actions are needed. In this case authoritative and pacesetting may be best.

Each person is different, and it is important to understand the setting in order to implement the best method.

Ever been thrown under the bus at work? Were all the facts known and discussed before this occurred?

I am sure it happens in many companies all over the world, but it is an unnecessary, toxic aspect that needs to be removed.

All it does is remove trust and openness within a team that is supposed to be working towards a common goal. Often you cannot get that trust back. Respect is lost and rarely regained, and the team will lose its cohesiveness.

Leaders especially need to ensure all facts are known before jumping on the band wagon. Leaders doing this is far worse as they are in a role that others are to look up to. They are to set a good example, not contributing to the toxicity.

This can also occur in our personal lives as well. It isn't solely a work thing.

While leadership isn't always or even usually easy, some leaders make situations harder. It is important to listen and talk less in many cases. A team is hired because of their talents and need to use those talents. Get varied opinions.

Always work to make oneself better as well as your team. Too often, especially as some rise through the ranks, they forget where they started. Never stop learning. There is usually something new to learn no matter how old you are or how long you have been in a position.
Be open.

Often folks think it is easy to be in a leadership role, and it is not.

There may be glaring weaknesses but also obvious strengths. It is important that we acknowledge our weaknesses and learn from them and grow. Not working on improving your weaknesses will cause long term damage to yourself as a leader but your teams' relationship with you.

Not everyone is suitable to be in a leadership role and it's not always to admit that.

Leaders need to empower their team as often it's the team who succeeds and not one person.

When employees are empowered they feel, generally speaking, more satisfied at work and more confident.

The opposite is true when they are watched over their shoulder, or if delegated to do something and the boss comes in and does it anyways.

Folks are hired in a role. The experienced ones especially need to be allowed to perform in that role. Training and mentorship is important, most certainly at the beginning, but why have folks in the position if they are not allowed to do it.

I have had plenty of people get promoted under me but I don't pretend to think that was all me. It was their initiative and hard work that drove them to succeed. I just encouraged along the way.

That is what leadership should do. Encourage and not stifle. Empower your team. Trust them to get the task done.

We often learn from failures and opportunities. Lessons learned makes us stronger.

Leadership in any company is a driving force behind its success, but as with all things, we are human and make mistakes.

Owning the mistake is important and learning from it.

Ensuring the properly sized workforce has the tools and training they need to succeed at any task is also important. Putting blame on others when it is your responsibility is one of many reasons why employees lose faith in leadership and end up moving on.

There are times where folks let their job title go to their head, expecting immediate respect. While in business, the hierarchy and leadership positions are means to be followed, respect is something that rarely is immediate.

Positions/Job Titles should not be the catalyst to respond to email requests or other business. Every position in a company should be respected. Respect goes both ways.

One thing often overlooked for a leader is to be technically proficient. You may be a great leader, but you need to understand what is going on around you. Employees look to leadership for guidance and instructions, which may be difficult if you have no idea what is going on or how's it's done.

Also, as a leader it is important not to waste employees' time when you may be able to do something or get something yourself. Delegation may be needed at times but isn't always the answer.

A good to great leader started as a follower. They also work to create more leaders, not followers.

Aristotle spoke on this over 2,000 years ago and it is as relevant now as then, if not more so.

Remember to be humble, loyal to your team, listen, learn, and check your ego at the door.

Quiet Manager.

The opposite of a micro manager, a quiet manager will give employees space to work, to breathe and be free try things.

It builds trust with the team knowing you have faith in their ability to complete tasks.

As with everything, there are positive and negatives to it. Just don't be too hands off, too distant. Be available to assist, mentor and provide resources.

Allow employees to do what they are there to do.

Summary

Leadership is a tough job to have. It takes effort, conviction, knowledge, patience, skill, intelligence, caring and so many more attributes.

A leader or boss can have none of these and still succeed, but generally through force and fear. That is not how a great leaders commands respect, and the teams trust, motivation and loyalty.

A goal should be to achieve greatness, not a title alone without what makes it great. Titles are empty and temporary. Be someone who looks back with positive thoughts on how you impacted their life. Be someone who is talked about in a positive way because you helped, mentored, guided and impacted people positively.

Chapter 3
Planning & Structure

Planning is critical in life, but very important in a business. If you don't plan, you plan to fail.

Every company is structured differently, but what is important is that the employees within a company understand who they work for as well as what the goal is to achieve. You would think that is straight forward, but it isn't always. That will often drain an employee of energy and creativity, create chaos and drive employees away from a workplace built in silos with no communication and guidance.

Next are thoughts on this vital topic, in no particular order.

Lately it seems that companies are short term planning and not long-term planning.

Both are needed of course but making short term decisions without thinking long term impact can have serious negative consequences. There have been plenty of articles in the news on this, some of which I have posted.

Leaders need to look at the forecast of activities, of workload and of history. We often forget about history and that can hurt both a company but also people as a society.

I am a student of history and I try to use lessons learned in my life. That doesn't happen as often as it should as we often repeat failures from the past. You see this in business and politics all the time, let alone in our personal lives.

A business making a rash decision to cover a short-term plan at the expense of the long term will certainly not help. Also, not using what has worked in the past for future, long term planning is foolish. If it worked why throw it away unless requirements have changed.

Shooting from the hip, making quick and rash decisions will always come with risks. You must live with that as a business or in your personal life.

It is up to us to make the best choice we can in our short time on this planet, whether we are the decision maker or those impacted.

Understanding current workload, tasks and future work will put companies in a good position to provide what their current and future customers need.

Eliminating positions is not always the answer to saving money. It can and does backfire with companies. There are a number of ways to improve financials without always shooting from the hip and laying off people.

Lessons Learned.

Whether at work or in our personal lives, if we do not learn from our successes and certainly our failures or missteps, we will be doomed to repeat the negative aspects.

We should want to continually succeed, even in small ways, so using what we have done in the past that worked should be the formula to use.

Outside of ourselves though, we should also help others succeed through our lessons learned.

Think the 5 P's as part of planning. Without proper planning there could be a very good chance of poor performance for your client/customer.

Additionally, it can simply cause chaos and inefficiency with the workforce leaving them stressed and worn out for no reason.

Proper planning is a win win.

Planning.

Whether for companywide, portfolio, program, project or in our personal lives, it is important we plan things out.

The right people need to be involved, to include Quality & Safety, with the right knowledge for everyone to do their part. Additionally, it also needs to be the right time and on time once started.

While some issues you can find online as examples for when plans fail may be funny, they are also costly as well as a nuisance. They can also cost lives.

Failure should not generally be considered a negative situation, although it often is. It is instinctive to not want to failure, to be embarrassed by it. We all want to be successful in what we do.

It is important though to keep learning from mistakes, improving each time, innovating towards success.

History is replete with examples of repeated failures that became outstanding successes.

Keep at it.

While planning is fundamental in what we do at work and inputs and requirements are generally an important part of it, what is important in the end is the output and outcome.

Too often the inputs can be micromanaged. If the outcome is positive, the outputs are compliant and on time, then it is a success.

While we can use Lean in the workplace to improve upon the inputs, we need to remember that we are not robots. You can get to a point where all the enjoyment is taken away, which is often limited as is.

For a business to be successful, planning is a big part of it. Know what you need, your client/customer requirements, and get the right people in place to make what you put in place work and maintain it through checks and balances.

Communication is another important element to be successful and often times underutilized.

Lastly, never forget about looking for improvements. Often, we get used to the way things are when we should see it as they could be.

Be open to the possibility.

Lessons Learned are often an underrated tool companies can use. Companies can become so big, and departments focused only on their own status that no one passes ideas around. Documenting Lessons Learned from projects or tasks can help others learn from the good or bad that developed. It can also help to remind you for a future project or task so you can continually improve.

Planning is critical for the success of any business. Poor Planning = Poor Outcome. A picture I have had in my office for a decade now reminds me of that. Putting stress on Colleagues, Customers and Clients due to last minute deadlines, changes or procrastination will create a chaotic, toxic workplace.

When everything is urgent, nothing is.

It is important that urgency be used when it is real and truly needed.

When everything is treated as an emergency or urgent, it is either because of poor planning or a lack of prioritizing.

It is vital that leadership properly prioritize tasks as to not unnecessarily overwhelm and stress out their employees. Leaders should understand if their employees become vocal and not slap them down (metaphorically speaking).

While procrastination is never good, a culture of false urgency will simply break down the team.

Having clear roles & responsibilities, while also keeping tasks on point and not constantly changing are musts. Change for the sake of change or constantly changing how work is done is not good change.

Micromanaging a professional staff will also never end well.

There is good stress at work, contrary to beliefs, when expectations are known for handling the work load which includes true urgent tasks.

Should we set our goals high or realistic?

That is difficult because we often want top tier goals, but make them so high they cannot be feasibly reached.

It is important to be realistic when we set goals because they should be attainable and not considered a failure if we can't meet them regardless of how much we try.

Are you committed? Are there obstacles/limitations to consider?

Plan it out well, researching what you can do. Stretch yourself, just don't overwhelm yourself or others.

It should be a goal of any company to have high performance teams.

It should be a goal of an employee to want to be a part of a high-performance team.

It takes the Sr. Leadership to establish that culture.

It always starts with open and clear communication and reachable goals to build trust from.

Giving employees a voice and praise will give them the opportunity to be a part of the company and give ideas that can positivity grow the company.

Break out of silos and work together, forging bonds between teams that will create a high performance company.

Be willing to put time and effort into the employees, giving them training and education opportunities.

If a company wants to be the best for their client/customer, get the best and cultivate to keep and grow the best. Mentor and build relationships that will stand the test of time.

Success isn't always easy. It takes a lot to make it work. Whether in our personal lives, or a business which has multiple functions working together.

Keep striving for goals, meeting requirements, breaking boundaries and one step at a time you will reach success.

In a large company the organization may have people working directly and indirectly for leadership.

This can be complicated at times but when managed properly can be an asset.

A straight line means you work directly for that person. They generally approve time sheets, complete performance reviews and give direct requests to be followed.

Dotted line means that while that person doesn't generally approve time sheets and may not play a part in performance reviews, they send requests to be completed. Often it is for projects, reports, deliverables that may be needed and tracking of progress for certain requirements.

This relationship entails cross communication and collaboration and can be beneficial to a company.

While dotted line may be considered secondary, it is still important and often vital when implemented to ensure various tasks are completed.

It is important though that roles, tasks, limitations and boundaries are set at the beginning to have everyone involved understanding clearly what is needed and required.

It should be a team effort and not an adversarial or combative relationship. This structure will often allow those involved to learn from one another to the benefit to themselves and the business.

I don't like the word quit. But with that said, it is important to know when to shut a project down if it isn't working, moving on from something if it isn't working for you and just understand when enough is enough.

In business it is important to know when to stop sinking money into something that is not materializing.

We all have breaking points in our lives and we should not consider it quitting to move to the next phase or step in our lives.

Summary

Planning is fundamental for any company, team, or project to have established because without it there will be no idea how to succeed, what will be needed, who will be involved, and chaos will ensue.

If a company and its Sr. Leaders within expect to have a cohesive team, it is important that they structure their organization that makes sense. Clear lines of authority with clear lines of understanding is a must to have a successful team.

In all this, communication is the driving force.

Chapter 4
Experts, Ambition, Motivation & Vision

It is important to mold and mentor those who have the interest and capability to become experts in their fields. Becoming an expert takes time, experience and knowledge. Leadership needs to support this and allow those interested to grow in their fields and not hold them down.

There are plenty of motivational gurus seen across social media and coaches that are available. Often it feels like the posts and ideas are empty ideas and not fit to our individual lives. It is up to each person to determine what motivates themselves. If not interested, external influences will not matter no matter how good the advice is. The drive must be within us in order to succeed.

Vision is an important part of a business that Sr. Leadership needs to develop and implement. Those within a company that has a vision statement, needs to understand their part to play in achieving the vision set forth by leadership. If not, the vision will not come to fruition and will be empty words. There are far too many empty words in this world of ours, so it is important to eliminate that through thoughtful action.

Next up are some thoughts on this, in no particular order.

Where have all the experts gone?

I saw a video once concerning this topic and it brought up an interesting point.

There are a lot of leaders in companies, but many couldn't do the work of the people below them. They are in management but that is it. They can probably lead but wouldn't necessarily be considered a subject matter expert in a certain field.

Innovation is often driven by experts. They look at the current task and processes and work to make it better, more efficient. This takes experience in certain aspects, tools and roles to implement.

Cross training and continually learning and expanding understanding also improves experience.

It takes time and effort to become an expert, but experts once known also need to be properly utilized. Utilized, not abused.

Companies need more experts which are leveraged for a stronger and more creditable business for current and future clients/customers.

Training is vital to the success of a business and its employees, but even more important is effective training. Too often a sign in sheet is passed around to document training without ensuring that the employees understand. That is where leadership comes into play.

Secondly, training by itself does not prevent issues as we all may forget a step and forget to fall back on the process in which we are to follow.

Ambition.

We often have it when we are younger as we are starting out in the business world.

Not always, but sometimes, we lose that ambition as we get older. While we want to drive to do things, to have things when we are younger thinking we have the world in the palm of our hand and long life ahead, we realize as we get older how short life is. We often see, looking back, how much that we missed in our ambition.

Each person is different. Different environment, different goals, different abilities. Don't let anyone take away your ambition but also understand that your ambition may change over time and may not always align with those around you.

Take time to look around.

Ambition, especially when we are young, is the goal to strive to for more. More hours at work to get that promotion, more prestige, both at work and in turn our personal lives.

With that said, the prestige, the titles, the possessions accumulated may come at a cost of time and relationships. Often at times as you get older you find you wish you had that time back to develop relationships and more.

Understand your goals and ambitions to know what you want and what the cost will be.

Motivation comes in many forms.

Motivation affects our work life and our personal life. We are motivated to do different things in both and at different times in our life.

We may be motivated to travel, to start a hobby, to volunteer, and at work we may need different motivation to stay productive.

Sometimes, especially recently with the uncertainty we often face, financial motivation is a main motivator.

It could be the thought of promotion, other awards or praise. It could be wanting a safe, secure quality workplace to work in. It could be something within that just makes you feel good.

If employees are not motivated they will become disengaged and will often look elsewhere.

Companies spend more looking for new employees than working to keep current, successful employees.

It is important that leadership find ways to motivate employees.

Now if a company only will treat employees as numbers, there isn't much to be done with the current leadership, but turnover will cost companies more from their bottom line over time.

Building trust, having transparent and open communication and clear, achievable goals are just the first steps towards a motivated team.

We should all want a positive workplace to thrive in.

In the end a business is there for its client/customer and a strong workforce, motivated to be there, will make a successful operation.

I see on various social media sites folks saying how easy something is to achieve and life is easy.

I get the mindset behind it. Motivation is important, but so is reality.

Life isn't easy. Each day is met with different challenges. Some days are great, good, okay, bad & terrible, sometimes all mixed up.

Our lives are like a mountain range.

Beautiful to look upon but depending on if we are climbing up, or climbing down, will determine what we face. Either way each day is a challenge that we face, hopefully with an optimism to make it, ourselves and those around us better. It is a daily task that we may not always achieve in a positive manner, but it is important we never stop trying.

You should always have a sense of purpose and a reason for being whether in our work life or personal life. Find your passion.

Short term vs long term vision.

There is research available online from studies that show due to short term thinking and a profit taking approach, long term success and company culture paid the price. Employee morale fell and they became disengaged and returns fell.

It is important to not forget about the big picture as well as what the client/customer wants. Putting people over profits will generally harm a company long term, as well as their reputation.

There must be a better way.

Vision is important for a company and leadership to drive towards achieving success for themselves as a business, but ultimately the client/customer.

A vision statement are only words unless put into practice and followed.

It needs everyone's active participation in order to work. Employees need to understand and believe in it and that comes from leadership through inspiration.

Communication as always is important, along with accountability, for the vision to be implemented properly.

Having a vision is not enough. It needs to be actioned. But first it needs to be shared.

Visions require collaboration, discussion along a team to make it work. The team will be the one to make it work.

Get into details. The big picture alone is not enough.

Without the team on board, understanding the goal, the vision may not succeed. Often it takes more than the one who created to idea to make it successful.

The why something needs to be done needs to come before the how and what to do. Vision and inspiration.

Summary

When we are younger and starting off our careers there is a high level of ambition and motivation to achieve great things in life. We will often forgo certain aspects of our lives to achieve success.

Later in life, often when we have become experts in our fields, that high level of ambition and motivation wanes. We discover, that as life is short, so too are opportunities we may have missed on our journey up the ladder.
Do your best to balance life and work to not have regrets later in life. You should not have to sacrifice your life for a job.

Chapter 5
What is Important & the Goal?

What is important at work? What are the goals for the company and the team? If the goals are not known and everything is important, there will be chaos.

Achieving a high-level vision for the company is one thing, but the day to day goals is another. To remove doubt, confusion, chaos and stress, it is important that goals are known by employees, especially if they are to be held to them for monthly, quarterly or annual targets.

If you have employee evaluations, there should not be any surprises when that time arrives.

Next are thoughts on importance and goals.

Importance.

What is important to you?

At work it is often the mission. The focus is on whatever your function does in your company for the client/customer.

In doing this there are often elements overlooked, ignored or just missed.

Quality, Safety, Environmental, Health, Security, and more are sacrificed to get the mission done when they should be part of the mission, dependent on the job.

Don't have time for that because I have a priority request from a customer to do x, y, z. I can ignore this because it is not important at the moment, even though it is and will come back to bite them in the behind.

In the end it is about priorities, importance, accountability and what people are held to in order to get accomplished their list of tasks. Sometimes we have too much on our plate. I know. We may have to pick and choose certain things. I get it.

We must do our utmost to be the best we can be each day and ask for help when needed. On a team it takes support. Solo it takes proper tasking and scheduling to stay on point.

In our personal lives there is a whole other set of what is important.

Don't let certain elements distract us from what really matters in life. We don't take money and things with us when we leave this plane of existence.

Cherish time with people, places and moments.

Whether you are a leader or not, if you expect a certain outcome for a task/assignment that you need from someone and didn't give proper guidance/direction, you will get what you get.

It is important, most especially from leadership, that clear direction is given. If not, the one doing the work will be confused, frustrated and may give an end result that is less than ideal.

If questions are asked and ignored, again you will get what you get.

Leaders especially should not demean anyone when they are not being leaders and doing what they should and mentoring and guiding.

If none of this is happening the leader is not doing their job and their employees will never meet expectations that are not clearly outlined.

How can anyone function in that situation? Why would they and why should they?

People in leadership are there to support, to help employees grow. Often people in these roles forget that and sometimes some may not care about that. Not an ideal work environment to thrive in and even survive in and the customer will feel it.

Having open communication where all parties talk and work as a team is the only way to properly succeed. Shutting each other out will never work.

Summary

Far too often priorities are swayed to less than important matters while issues affecting the customer/client is ignored. Priorities are in the eye of the beholder and with those in power, for better or worse.

It takes the right people, in the right positions to make a positive impact, and each company and each team will be different. Goals should be achievable in a time frame that makes sense with targets that can be met.

Be S.M.A.R.T., act S.M.A.R.T., and focus on the right things.

Chapter 6
Communication & Skills

Communication is the #1 aspect in our lives that is crucial at work, out in public and at home in our personal lives.

Not properly communicating will destroy relationships, give you a stagnant career and personal life and cause unnecessary strife and difficulties.

Communication is often not used correctly or even used, which leaves people blind, worried, stressed and out of touch with what may be going on around them. This is something that needs to be improved across the board all over the world.

Between hard skills and soft skills, both are important in our daily lives at work and outside. Soft skills though are often relegated to secondary status when they are just as important, if not more so.

Soft skills are what will get you through the day successfully and positively interact with colleagues and customers.

Next are some thoughts on this very important topic in all our lives, in no particular order.

Communication I have found has been an ongoing issue in all our lives, whether at work, home or out in public.

We all interpret things differently and react in different ways. It could be shown as confusion, frustration, annoyance, anger, irritation at the way the communication is perceived.

Whether it is reading an email/message, speaking with someone or being spoken at by someone, or body language, what we want to convey may not always be interpreted the way we wish.

In business and especially Quality, we try to get across the importance of meeting the client/customer requirements. This can be through meetings, emails, message boards, audits and more.

We point out perceived fallacies in the workplace, suggest improvements, work to train, educate and mentor those who need assistance with understanding the intricacies of compliance, continuous improvements and customer satisfaction to name some.

And with even the best intentions in mind, actions will be taken in a negative way by the workforce.

We will never please those around us 100% of the time. All of us will fall short of that mark.

It is important that all parties are open to listening, to learning.

Not everyone can do every aspect of every job in the workplace, even after being taught, explained, shown and given hands on training. Some in the workplace will be stronger and weaker in some areas.

It is important that leadership use the right talent in the right places. Together with open communication, the team as a whole will be stronger to give their client/customer excellent service every day.

It is how communication is given and received that will ultimately gain or retract support for an initiative.

Quality is one area that needs support by everyone to succeed.

Cross Tell. Cross Communication

It doesn't happen as often as it should.

Functions within a company are often happy in their separate silos. That will inhibit a company's growth by stunting knowledge that one function may have that could improve another.

It all starts with communication and a willingness to reach out and reciprocate.

Company goals for the client/customer will often take more than one section to achieve. Working together as a team with clear objectives will make for a winning strategy.

No need on hide from each other.

This also goes for those in the same field from different companies and countries to further improve their field.

Heard it through the grapevine.

While a good song, the phrase is negative in other aspects.

When this occurs in the workplace it is often because of uncertainty and unclear or a complete lack of direction, guidance, and overall communication blackout from leadership.

This leads to rumors, whispers, uncertainty, stress and negative conditions that affect the employees, impact work and may certainly impact the client/customer.

Communication is often the #1 weakness in companies and life in general. With so many communication choices available you'd think we would better at it now, but we often are not.

Transparency and openness are the main drivers toward trust. Without it, teams within a business will crumble and eventually the entire company from collapse from within.

If that is the goal, keep at it. If not, change the direction toward clear communication.

Here is a serious thought and question we all probably face in our daily lives.

Why won't they respond to my text, email, message, phone call?

Why are they not paying attention to what I send?

With communication so easy now, why does it seem harder than ever?

This can happen to friends, family, colleagues & strangers.

Is the message wanted? Important? Needed to be responded to by a certain date/time? Is it relevant?

Are you being ghosted, simply ignored because the other party doesn't care?

Is too much information being conveyed in the correspondence?

It is important to understand the context but is also important that both parties be open and understand the need for the communication.

If it is at work and an email or message is being sent on important information/updates, it shouldn't be ignored. It could either jeopardize the operations or because time being wasted later. The receiving party needs to respond and if needed, ask questions. Ignoring is simply bad business.

In our personal lives there may be times where we may not want to answer a message from a friend or loved one for a variety of reasons, but ignoring the message and attempt to communicate won't improve the situation.

There are always going to be outliers, unique situations, but communication needs to go both ways and not ignored by one party.

You cannot stay in a communication silo and expect to succeed alone in this world, whether business or personal.

Communication.

It remains elusive to many, frustrating to most and difficult for some.

Why though?

There are so many ways we can communicate now. Maybe it is communication overload?

I don't know. I just see a lot of ignoring of communication that is available in the workplace.

Whether it is the company or a department sending an email out or using a message site/app like Teams, or something like Yammer (Engage), Slack or Meet.

It can be a topic brought up in a meeting.

After using all that, whatever the topic was, the issue remains because no one listened, or cared. No one may have passed the word to others as well.

There are so many variables but without reading, listening, comprehending, asking questions, following up, progress will always be an arm's length away. Just out of reach.

Whether at work or in our personal lives, let's take the extra effort to get better at communication in both giving and receiving.

Communication continues to be an important element often ineffectively used in our lives.

It is important that we have open channels to use to talk to each other at work, but also in our personal lives.

Listening is just as important in communication but also effective understanding of the discussion is key.

If you leave the discussion not clear on the intent or there was an impasse, you are in limbo.

Being ignored is also detrimental to any relationship.

Transparency and clarity of what is needed and what is occurring keeps employees engaged at work. When emails, messages, verbal comms are garbled, unclear, or just plain evasive, you will breed doubt, and possible contempt in the workplace.

That will not be conducive to an environment that will flourish for the client/customer.

There may be plenty of times, whether at work or in our personal lives, people will not listen. They may have their reason, but it sets us roadblocks in communications and inhibits growth in relationships.

Being in a leadership position does not necessarily mean you will be automatically listened to. It's important that communication is two way and open.

If a leader constantly shuts down their employees, doesn't listen, take advice and act upon it, it will quickly become one-way communication and information will stop flowing.

There may be plenty of others who will listen and take the advice.

How often have you found something that has changed when you go to do something at work? Was it communicated? Is it documented even? How do you know what to do to be successful?

Far too often things are done on the fly and/or without cross communication and chaos can ensue when it is implemented without controls in place. Don't put the cart before the horse. Do what is right from the beginning.

An effective Business and Functional Leadership structure will not have a silo mindset.

Open communication is important and cross communication and assistance is vital to the success of a business and its employees.

There may be best practices out there you can use from someone else because in the end a business is there for its employees, customers and clients.

Strive for excellence.

Life is challenging.

Making life more challenging with unnecessary actions just makes it worse and is often pointless.

At work, many companies have many layers of bureaucracy, slowing work to a crawl, making decisions slow, difficult, or nonexistence. Bottlenecks cause further issues with single point failures, time wastes and simply extra steps and people/departments to go through that hinders the workplace.

Efficiency should be the rule. Layers should be removed, bottlenecks eliminated through redundancy (backups), middle people removed, and extra steps cut out.

Functions within a company should work together and not butt heads. A company which infights, will not prosper and will wilt and collapse over time as people will get tired of the politics and leave.

It can be no different at home. People like drama and may on purposely bring it into their lives.

It may be tolerable on tv, or movies, but I know I speak for myself when I say drama can stay out of my life. That goes for both work and home life.

Life has enough challenges that throw us curveballs. We should not give ourselves and others more difficulties.

As with everything, communication is a big part of this, and it is generally one of the top 3 issues in our lives, especially at work.
Accountability is another, and those who are unnecessarily difficult need to be held accountable.

Let's make our days a little bit better by getting better at this. Small steps in the right direction will get us there, even if slowly.

Soft Skills.

While often times hard skills are what is looked for by companies, training can often solve that part.

Soft skills are more challenging and are quite important for people to have from the get go.

Ideally soft skills need to be taught to us when we are young and then develop them over years.

They will often make up our personalities and will impact how we interact with coworkers.

No matter what our age, it is important to keep working on soft skills to continually improve how we effectively perform at work and even in our personal lives.

Listening is a soft skill not everyone has.

It is important that when listening that you listen to understand and not just reply.

There are plenty out there that like to talk, talk, talk, but that is not conducive to an environment where ideas should be shared, opinions matter and people feel engaged and their thoughts listened to whether at work or in personal lives.

Summary

Communication is the foundation of any relationship. Without it, life will be much more difficult than it needs to be. Learning how to properly communicate should start when we are young, but there may be times as adults that it is beneficial to go through classes on the subject. As we all grow up in different environments, different cultures, there will be times where we face obstacles we are not used to.

Over the decades what was once acceptable or tolerated is no longer allowed in the workplace, home or public. As with all things, evolution occurs that we must adapt to. People evolve, language evolve, circumstances change. We must adapt to survive in the world as we social creatures, even those of us who may be introverts.

While we go through school and learn on the job skills, take certification and licensing training, soft skills are what will get us through the day easier.

Chapter 7
Ego, Confidence & Emotional Intelligence

The line between ego and confidence can be thin, especially to those around you. You may feel you are confident when others would call you egotistic.

Emotional intelligence is an underrated skill these days and often overlooked as required. Regardless of older mindsets and business models out there, emotional intelligence is a key aspect to understanding your team and leading the proper way, by putting your employees first. Next are some thoughts on this touchy subject, in no particular order.

It is important to understand the difference between ego and confidence.

I am sure in our lives we have faced people with a big ego and nothing to back it up.

We have probably encountered many quiet people that exude confidence.

You don't need to be loud or an extravert to have an ego and quiet people or introverts can be confident. Don't let these definitions define you and don't peg people into a certain category.

No matter the role or position in a company or life in general, it is important to not allow ego to get in the way of learning, listening and growing.

We all have something to learn from one another throughout our lives.

Be open to it.

It is a fine line between confidence and arrogance, and together we can stay on the side of confidence.

Too often titles go to one's head.

We must remember that titles are temporary, and we generally started at the bottom and worked our way there.

It is a leader's job to assist their team in their rise through the ranks, not hinder it.

Forcing someone to do a task because of a title won't necessarily get the best results.

When the culture or accountability is not strong and folks do as they wish in a company, the result may be the customer/client getting less than desired or no products/services. At this point they could demand money back or the product/service they expected, on the dime of the company providing it. They could also pass along to other companies the less than desirable work and the company reputation take a hit.

It is important and vital that leadership takes seriously the quality of work they provide, processes needed to be successful and advise given by those in the position to help.

Ego should never be involved.

Unless social media is blowing things out of proportion, it seems that emotional intelligence in leadership has nosedived off a cliff.

It feels that the business world has taken steps backwards in time.

While companies are often revered in good times, how they treat their employees and clients/customers in difficult times is more telling of the culture they have.

Any good to great leader in the world needs to have a higher level of EQ, unless you are planning to be a maleficent dictator, James Bond villain, or other such character.

There are plenty of free tests online you can find to see where you fit.

We are a social species, even when some of us are introverts. It is important to understand one another, whether at work or our personal lives. As a leader this is even more important and EQ is something that can be worked on.

If you are not interested in emotional intelligence and how it can positively impact people as well as in the other direction, I feel sorry for you. That goes double for those in leadership roles because you play a vital role in people's lives.

Emotional Intelligence.

Even though this is something that all leaders, and really all employees should work on.

From both a standpoint that you need to control your emotions at work, be self-motivated and treat fellow colleagues well, leaders need to exude these characteristics more so.

It is important to know and understand your fellow employees and read their emotions as they will play a part in the work being done.

We are not robots and a workplace will be more successful when employees are treated as people and not a number.

Whether in person or virtual, it is important to have that social connection with the team because like it or not, even for us inverts, we are social beings.

This skill is also important in our personal lives. There are tests you can take for free online to see where you fall in your EI/EQ and where you can work to improve.

What makes a happy employee? What can a business do better out there?

I can certainly see work-life balance as an issue. Being able to turn off work and relax our minds and not forced to stress or worry about work 24/7.

Accountability from Sr. Leadership on down is another, which will be another post. Positive and known work expectations. Piling on work with short timetables never really helped anyone.

Micromanaging rarely works. If you hire creative and talented folks, let them do what you hired them for, right?

Respect and Acknowledgement of employees certainly doesn't hurt. It's a two-way street in the world of business and personal lives.

If you want Quality & Safety in the workplace, it takes effort to build that culture and it's the employees and leadership working together who make it happen.

Summary

Cutting out ego in the workplace will create a more open, transparent, honest, healthy environment for the team to thrive. Ego simply destroy teams and companies, especially when there are too many ego's in Sr. Leadership across the board.

Emotional intelligence is a skill needed these days that is vastly underutilized across companies and Sr. Leaders. Whether on purpose or not, not using this skill maintains a gap between leadership and the workforce, causing mistrust and uncertainty. It takes setting aside ego to adopt the practice of emotional intelligence.
Let's do better together.

Chapter 8
Understanding the Team & Teamwork

It is important for any leader in any position within any company to understand their team. Whether you inherit a team or build your own, knowing and understanding those under your charge is a key to your success.

Teamwork. Whether you believe you can do it all or not, a team is often required to be successful to meet the customer/ client goals. Most teams may have a superstar, but each member of a team has certain abilities and strengths that make the task easier.

Next are some thoughts on this critical topic for leaders, in no particular order.

With so many companies these days focusing strictly on the bottom line at the expense of their people and sometimes customers, even while making millions and billions of dollars, it is important that leadership not then complain when about the consequences.

If money and hours are being strictly watched and enforced, you can then not complain if work is not getting done or that calls are not being taken after hours or even immediately during the day.

Forcing an overburdened workload onto someone because overtime will not be paid out, spots won't be filled, or expecting an illogical amount of work to get done in a short period of time will have dire consequences long term.

Telling the workforce from employees to lower and middle managers that week and week and month after month, hours are being watched, workload & outputs are being watched and it is an act of congress to ever get more hours is most of the time demoralizing. I don't know too many people that enjoy working under a microscope and in a constantly hectic environment. More power to those that do. It will eventually wear a person down mentally, physically and emotionally.

Suddenly, one day you and/or your team are the problem if you want to take some time off or suddenly it is a problem that there supposedly weren't enough people available to possibly assist a hypothetical internal or external customer on a slow holiday week (And there probably were enough people, but leadership wasn't paying attention).

In a leadership position, one should have the knowledge and experience to understand what can get done in a certain amount of time with a certain amount of people, generally speaking. Each person works at a different speed and leadership needs to understand that and not abuse it. Employees in turn also should not abuse the situation and work to their best ability, communicating any issues they have.

If a leader does not support the team in order to succeed, they should not be in a leadership role, period. There are too many leaders, seen on far too many social media sites and accounts, that are out there abusing people for no apparent reason. A power trip and inflated ego will only get you so far in life. Some may get further in life than others, but at the end of the day, at the end of a life, was it worth it?

Since the COVID 19 pandemic, the job market has seen some interesting times.

The great resignation, followed by quiet quitting, then loud quitting, then quiet hiring and now the latest and most insidious is quiet firing.

Employees make a business succeed through their positive actions for whatever the customer wants in their given business.

When the employees are neglected, ignored, shunned and generally treated poorly, the effect will become a negative output for the customer.

Compliance and Safety, among other important attributes, will falter in this environment and in the long term cost money, reputation and possibly lives.

No sane company and leadership structure should ever want that.

Ever heard of the ask, don't tell approach?

It is a way to get your team to think about ideas, actions, plans instead of you telling them to do x, y, z.

It makes them part of the decision making, giving them a chance to make a difference.

It also lends the team some accountability and autonomy in the decisions that affects them.

As a leader you aren't seen as barking orders but getting advice from your teams experience to influence decision making.

This is also how you grow the team and they get upward mobility with promotions through the leadership decision making experience offered.

While it would be ideal that everyone respect each other, that is not the case.

Respect is a powerful element in our lives and is often earned over time, not granted at a request.

You will see varying opinions on it from respect should be earned to respect should be automatically given and everything in-between.

Respect should go both ways and there are different levels of respect from the polite to revered.

Firstly, be humble. Respect will rarely work if there is a level of intimidation and demand. It shouldn't necessarily be something that is entitled.

Everyone should get at least basic decency from others no matter the situation.

Lead by positive example, teach, mentor, coach others and listen.

Respect will happen naturally.

You should be able to ask for assistance at work.

If you can't there are issues.

We often don't want to ask for help because we will feel stupid or inadequate, but none of us are perfect or know everything.

We can all learn something new from time to time as it helps keep us stagnant. Collaboration is also a good thing.

It also shouldn't matter what position title we have. Learn from those around you and foster that type of environment.

Teamwork and Leadership.

To be successful you need both working in harmony.

You need a clear, concise plan and path forward for a team to work from and a goal to work towards, and leadership needs to support the team to achieve it.

Members of a team needs to contribute, providing their piece to the overall plan and goal.

Transparency and integrity are key to staying on course. Leadership needs to motivate, inspire and provide resources when needed.

Responsibility falls on every member of the team.

Communication as always is a vital aspect to teamwork.

No one should want to fail, so work to succeed.

Appreciation. Recognition. Gratitude.

These are all something we all crave from time to time. Whether it is at work or our personal lives.

It is just one element that if provided will keep the company morale up, turnover low and associated costs down.

It is though not always done and if done for employees, not always recognized by the ones who should be providing that recognition, gratitude and appreciation.

Have you helped a family member to do something and later down the road they ask and this time you may not be able to help? They quickly forget you helped them previously and lay on guilt.

Have you worked a big project that helped the company, it's employees and long-term time and potential costs was saved? Was it recognized at the time? If it was, was it the right people in the company? If so, have you faced a situation later on, maybe months or a few years later where that project is history and you are no longer seen as relevant even if you have been producing great work?

I see posts on various social media sites where people face this all the time in their lives.

It can be frustrating and demoralizing. Their efforts to communicate with leaders or others in the business are ignored, whether on purpose or not.
Communication is a perennial problem in life, and it can't only come from one side.

It makes you no longer want to put forth effort, to help, to spend time that in the end is possibly a waste in someone's eyes.

Companies, leadership and even coworkers need to band together and raise up great performers and just each other instead of beating employees down for every minor mistake.

We shouldn't be just numbers in a company and there are plenty of reports out there that shows this is a big problem in many companies that is costing trillions a year in lost productivity.

You often don't understand the value until you don't have it.

We can do better. We need to do better. It will take all of us to move in the right direction for the culture across the world to change.

Leadership should always want the best around them.

The team in the end is what makes something successful which achieves the goals and vision of the business.

If leadership goes out and hires the best they can find, they should then let them be successful. Give them freedom to succeed.

Don't become alienated, jealous or threatened of their capability.
Use their capability to enrich your life, whether it is at work or outside of it.

Why are there times when people don't want to speak up in a meeting?

Nervous, shy, language barriers, don't understand the answer or subject and afraid to give the wrong answer and be embarrassed?

Could be any of these or more.

Could also be the environment is not open to such discussion. Could be that the employees involved don't feel their answer or suggestion will be what their leadership is looking for. The leader (s) could be expecting something that is in their mind and no answer will quite match it.

There are times where more than one answer can be right.

Keeping a meeting positive and discussion open, and not negative, will allow those involved to know their ideas will be listened to and everyone is free to offer thoughts.

If not, expect a silent room and don't complain about it.

It is important that companies put the right people in the right positions. That isn't always easy. There will be times that an individual will be great at something but not have the capability to transfer that greatness into another role. It's also important to not always look within to hire. Time in a job doesn't always translate to capability for more.

We may not always like to hear it, but there are times we may reach our pinnacle and need to understand our boundaries. Often though we find that out after we find ourselves in a difficult situation.

This topic will tie into some future posts I will do this week and also some past posts already here.

It is important to utilize employees and not constrain them. Having a diverse team with a variety of abilities is important. While it is important to cross train, not everyone can do each other's tasks to the same degree.
We recruit folks to do a job/task, and we should help them grow and learn more through mentoring but allow them to do what they were hired for.

A business/workplace should always be willing to get diverse thoughts and opinions.

Give credit when credit is due and to the right person (s).

Too often we get lambasted for doing something wrong, even when we do a hundred good things. People are quick to blame and slow to praise. Should be the opposite.

Human nature or not, we need to break from that condition and change the culture at work and in our personal lives by crediting people for outstanding work.

Additionally, those who do great work need to speak up for themselves. Doing so doesn't make you arrogant, but it can be a fine line towards bragging, so you need to be careful.

Credit shouldn't be stolen by anyone.

Let's do better each day to praise those around us.

Single Point Failure.

It should be something that a business prevents. It is a known risk that can be easily mitigated by ensuring that others can perform a task or track an action in the absence of the primary individual.

When this is not in place the business opens itself up to issues from the client/customer.

Cross training, especially if you only have one person assigned to a role, is a necessity. There should never be an excuse that someone is on vacation, out on medical, or there was a sudden departure.

It is leaderships position to ensure there are backup plans and contingencies in the event of this.

One person, no matter how valuable, should never put a company, department, team in a bad situation.

I have seen this happen too often and it is an easy thing to fix most of the time.

Summary

As a leader, if you do not know and understand your team and what makes them tick, you will fail.

Teamwork is a critical element within any company. While there will be some superstars and those who work well alone, it will take a team of professionals working together to give the best results for the customer/client.

Leaders should not be expected to know everything, and they will and should surround themselves with knowledge. They should not denigrate their team for possibility having more knowledge than them. Use their knowledge to the benefit of the team, company and who you are there for, which is the customer/client.

One team, one fight.

Chapter 9
Delegating

It is important, whether you are in leadership or not, to understand the importance of delegating to help with the workload. It is not always easy, especially for those who are new to leadership, or feel uneasy asking fellow colleagues. A team, if strong, should have no issue helping each other.

The prime issue within companies, is the rise of an unstable workload that is too much for one person to handle due to cost cutting initiatives. It is difficult to delegate if there is no one else to help.

This is something that needs to be looked at for improvement, because it needs to be in order to have a workforce who feels they are respected, treated well, and seen.

Next are some thoughts on this, in no particular order.

Delegating.

It can be difficult for some leaders.

They may not want to let go.

Some may be stuck between a rock and a hard place, with their leadership expecting them to do tasks and then other times expecting it to be delegated. It also depends on the org structure and who there is to delegate to.

This is tied though to clear communication and clear expectations of roles and responsibilities.

Who to delegate to is also important because not everyone will be strong in every task. Even though delegated, it will fall on you to ensure it is done right. Be available to assist and answer questions if they arise.

Work as a team and not just pass the buck and workload for the sake of it or because you are in a senior role. That certainly won't foster trust and cooperation.

There will be times in life that no matter how good you are at juggling multiple activities, projects, tasks, etc., that you will not succeed 100% of the time.

There are levels of importance in what we do, whether at work or home. Focus needs to be on the requirements and often we are doing things that are not needed, expected by a customer, important at the time or just not a priority ever. Let those drop off and focus solely on the important stuff when it becomes too much.

It is important to look at the list of activities we are doing to see what is value added or not. Drop the wastes in your life.

Delegate when you can and makes sense.

Ask for help from those around you, if you are fortunate to have that choice.

Time is finite. Use it wisely.

While it may be ideal, not everyone in a leadership position is going to be able to do every task their people do.

While front line leadership may as they are the ones teaching, training and mentoring the staff, the higher you go up the ladder the more there is to monitor.

When this happens, you may get knowledge of activities through reports, but you will probably not be in the weeds doing the tasks.

I have touched on working in silos and bottlenecks in the operation before, but it is a topic that seems to be a continually issue in workplaces.

You do what you do, and I will do what I do.

Send me the plan and I will get around to it.

Both of these scenarios occur and both can be detrimental to a team and business.

For both communication is important and communication is usually the #1 issue in business and even in our personal lives.

Many functions within a company need to work together for the company as a whole to be successful. Break down the silos and talk to each other.

For bottlenecks, if there is only one person that can do something, it will cause issues in the long run. There always needs to be a backup because life happens.

And if a leader has tasks, plans, reports, whatever it may be waiting on them, it can hurt the team if it piles up and is either not dealt with or plans not communicated to other parties.

Delegate and empower when needed. A title without authority is useless and empowering others grows the next set of leaders.

A team should not suffer due to leadership, or lack of, and it goes the other way as well. A team needs to provide support for leadership.

If a team is tasked with too much, especially unnecessary tasks, it should be liked at for streamlining. A part of solving bottlenecks is to look at the operation to ensure it is running smoothly and even throughout the entire process.

A company should always be ready and looking for growth opportunities and be flexible and adaptive for it.

Summary

Delegating is not easy, especially for new leadership or certain situations where there is no one to delegate a task to even when you are in a leadership role.

When new to leadership you are used to doing what you have been doing, possibly for years. Letting go does not feel right, but once in a leadership role the tasks you did normally go to someone else, and you enter a mentorship role.

When you are not in leadership, and you have a strong team, delegating tasks within the team can help keep a balanced workload. Teamwork is required for this and this is where relationship building becomes important.

For delegating, the right people need to be chosen as not everyone can do everything at the same level. Sometimes this takes trial and error.

Chapter 10
Trust & Relationships

If you don't have trust with your employees as a leader and a team doesn't trust each other, the team will fail. Trust can take time and happens through action. If you don't show trust, you won't receive it.

For a team to be successful in the mission, they must be able to work with each other. Trust takes time and effort but is a fundamental piece to what makes teams work well. Building that trust should be a goal of any great leader and team.

If that effort is not the goal of a leader, they may not be in the right role.

Next are some thoughts on trust, in no particular order.

If the work environment is such that employees have to file away somewhere all the good work they are doing in order to show management, as a CYA action, the environment is not a good one.

Doing this takes time and effort on the employees part and simply shows a negative culture in place between leadership and everyone else.

You will never get the best out of people if they are constantly feeling the need to take time out of their day to cover their behinds with emails or documented information like slide shows, ad-hoc reports, etc. that are all in addition to the regular work.

There should be clear ideas of tasks and duties needed which leadership should be aware of and the end results/outputs monitored as needed.

Any business needs to have a mutual understanding as well as trust between leadership and employees in order to succeed.

Trust and respect are two things that are important in our life.

Doesn't matter if it is at work or in our personal lives

Both though take time and are not immediate. They can both be lost and can take time to regain.

They also take both parties to put in place. If only one side exhibits trust and respect, it will not work.

Morale will suffer.

Trust and respect come from integrity, competency and intent. Intent is important because, especially with leadership, it is important to be transparent, open and clear with colleagues.
Setting expectations and goals that can be met. Understanding current roles and not dismissing the team's efforts are steps in the right direction.

Works and actions are important from both sides.

Supporting the team is key because that is what leadership does.

Following through with commitments and being consistent with messages will help grow trust.

Admitting mistakes from both sides will also help as no one is perfect and we all learn from them, no matter our position in life.

Presence can occur whether in a remote work environment or in the office. It is important that leadership especially ensures they are present for their employees.

Presence is about building trust and openness with a team. It isn't just about taking command of a room or situation.

Having an environment where the team wants to talk and discuss ideas. Where listening is just as important as talking and acting.

Training through periodic workshops, hands on training or other forms, along with feedback is important.

Not being stuck on one way to do things by being open to new ideas will remove rigidity that can destroy teams.

Be the leader your team needs, not just a boss or person with a title.

Is it better to be liked, respected or effective at work?

Maybe all 3?

It is important that while most want to be liked, and respect is generally earned over time, to be effective as a leader and employee alike, effectiveness in the job will require a bit of everything.

Having skills, expertise, thoughtful, willingness to learn, willing to be wrong, open to communicate, listening to those around you, being trustworthy, having integrity, being open to change are just some qualities and abilities that will get you there.

Some are good at talking while others are better at doing. Some are good at both.

Being open and willing to make the right decisions is important and may not make you friends and sometimes may be hard. It is important though that decisions are made wisely with all known facts and angles reviewed.

Summary

Without trust the team, and in turn the company, will not be successful. If you have a team or company full of people who are watching their backs, the focus will not be on the goal of achieving the customer/client's requirements and needs.

This should not be a goal for any company or leader. If it is, as I have stated elsewhere, leadership may not be their ideal role. If someone simply wants power for the sake of power, the future may not be bright for them. It will depend on who they are surrounded by and the level of tolerance they have.

Chapter 11
Accountability & Integrity

Accountability, as I have found over my years of working, is generally up there with lack of communication as the top problem area within companies.

Without accountability, it is essentially anarchy within a company or certainly feels that way. Anyone and everyone can get away with whatever they wish… except maybe you.

It takes Sr. Leadership in any organization to take this matter seriously, to include for themselves, for this to not be an issue and the structure of the business to be sound.

A fundamental, critical and important aspect of each of us is integrity. You don't have it, there will be problems. Regardless of our title and position in life, without integrity you are achieving meaningless results. You may not feel that now, or even while alive, but regardless of the afterlife, your impact on others will reflect through time.

Next are some thoughts on this important, critical subject.

Apologies and accountability. These two go hand in hand because one without the other is often meaningless.

A sincere apology will go a long way to mending a relationship. But empathy in the apology and follow on actions are what matters.

If you do not follow through with your apology, of course it is of no value but will hinder any possible future relationship.

Owning up to mistakes, taking concrete actions, following through and living the apology will be what mends the relationship.

If actions do not reflect words, there will never be trust, in nor particular order.

Accountability.

Outside of a lack of communication, it tends to be another top, hot button topic in both work and personal lives that is an issue.

The right people are not held accountable while others who are actually not responsible are.

How do you think morale and relationships will be when the environment is like that.

Recently in the business world, a company verbally took "responsibility" for the reason behind mass layoffs, although they are still making massive amounts of cash.

Where the accountability was needed was in actions by the Sr. Leadership of the company as they were the root cause of the issue.

Instead of putting in corrections to prevent a reoccurrence or find innovative solutions or actually taking more responsibility onto themselves, thousands are now out of work, wondering how they will pay bills and put food on the table.

This has been happening quite a lot lately.

Daily there are many out there at work being blamed for others failures. It is indicative of a failed culture and society as a whole. It permeates our lives even at home.

Accountability is really something that needs to be taught at a young age and worked on throughout our lives.

Mistakes happen. Own it and learn from it.

Others though should not have to pay for the lack of accountability for what they are not responsible for. It should be a work in progress for everyone.

Talk to each other like people and we may solve the lack of communication and accountability in time.

Accountability.

If you own a solution and it doesn't go your way, don't pass the blame to someone else. Own up to it.

Listening to advice may also keep the decision from going south. You may not know everything, even if you think you do. Listening to those around you, experts you may work with may make for more positive decisions.

A business cannot be successful with blame being thrown around. Stop throwing people, teams, departments under the bus. Listen more, talk less. Use knowledge around you instead of fearing it.

Work towards solution making and positive outcomes for the company and their client/customers.

The Quality you provide will improve over time because of it.

We should all be accountable in life, whether at work or at home.

When some are treated one way compared to another group in regards to accountability, it tends to bring to the organization a negative cloud of anger, spite and bitterness.

It is important that leadership holds the right people accountable for the right stuff, but also that accountability is equal and fair across the board. Not doing so will most certainly drive some away while making others who stay bitter, angry and no longer motivated to do their best.

It is not conducive to a positive environment in which the client/customers' requirements are being met. Proper accountability can and should be considered a positive situation.

Quality and Accountability. Two important topics that are inter-related.

Remember that Quality is doing the right thing when no one is looking.

Accountability starts with Sr. Leadership and building a positive culture is an important step in having a quality system that is compliant to the customer/client requirements. We all play a part, but it needs a kick start from the top.

Integrity.

Whether at work or in our personal lives, integrity makes or breaks relationships.

Without it, relationships will suffer and erode. Teams will break up and move on, families will suffer and friendships will fade.

Be honest and do what is right even when no one is looking.

Be responsible for your actions.

Be trustworthy and open.

Be respectful and considerate of others.

Help and not tear down people.

We can all do better each day, but it starts with looking within before critiquing and criticizing others.

Let's do our part to make the environment we live and work in a better place.

Without Integrity in the workplace from all employees, any system designed and implemented for the success of the company intended for the customer/client, will fail.

Summary

Integrity is something that is found within all of us. Some may repress it, but it is one of the fundamental pieces to what makes us each moral, and incorruptible in life. This isn't just for work, but in all aspects of our lives.

Accountability, I have found through experience, is usually one of the top three traits missing in the workplace across the world. It is often competing with Communication for the top spot.

The question is why?

Does it start when young? Is it taught in school? Is it learned at work? Is it to cover actions companies and teams don't want known?

We all make mistakes in life, but it is important we own them and learn from them and teach others through those lessons learned not to repeat them.

Transparency is often lacking in the business world. Ask any employee what is going on within their company and you may very well receive shrugged shoulders. That also builds or erodes trust within a company, which leadership may not see as an immediate problem, but it will impact the long-term vision and goals through attrition, lack of substance and will negatively impact the customer/client in the end.

Chapter 12
Loyalty & Transparency

Loyalty is a two-way street in life. Transparency goes along with loyalty because if you can't see what is going on, how can you trust the situation?

This is something important in all aspects of our lives, but at work, without these you will not have a cohesive team working in everyone's best interest.

Both loyalty and transparency have taken a beating in recent years in the business world, as both have been lost between employer and employee.

That has created many hostile workplaces and wary people, no longer trusting companies they either work in, or want to work in due to how they have treated past and current employees.

Layoffs are used as a tool that shouldn't be used as they currently are, which are weapons on its face is to save money, but often go back to the coffers of already rich companies.

There are many ways to save money and removing employees should be the last type of cost saving to look at, because in the Quality world there are many ways Lean can be used to streamline processes, systems and organizational structures. As I have worked on many projects that had hard and soft savings of millions of dollars, it takes an open mind, openness to innovation, teamwork, and a willingness to do what is needed to improve the workplace.

Next are some thoughts on this critical topic, in no particular order.

Loyalty.

It is an important element in our lives, especially in our personal lives. Friends and family will often help get us through our life. Even though we may think we do, we don't often go it alone. Support, giving and receiving is important.

At work loyalty is just as important as we spend 8, 10, 12 hours or more at it a day. You will often hear at work that we are a family because we spend more time at work than with our family. While the time part is true, work is work and family is family. There often comes a time where the desire to spend actual beneficial time with family, friends will replace the desire to be a workaholic. While treating work colleagues as a second family may or may not be okay dependent on views, actual family should never be forgotten.

Employees are often expected to be loyal to a company, to sacrifice time, energy, relationships and their health (mental/physical) to support it.

Companies have always laid off employees with no notice, but in recent years it has become prevalent and from many multi-billion dollar businesses. These have been difficult years and the lack of loyalty from many companies have left many wary.

How can anyone feel secure? That just elevates stress and sickness which has grown.

Technology has over the centuries replaced workers with machines. That is a part of advancements in our society. People though will always be the backbone of a business that will foster a culture of growth and success for its clients/customers.

Treating employees as a number or as a throwaway will cost companies more in the long run. Those who remain or future employees will never feel truly secure which will lead to a less than ideal environment to foster positive growth in the business.

How companies operate now needs to evolve in a positive direction and as more of the younger generation takes hold of positions of authority, I see that evolution occurring.

Making money is great, but not at the expense of our humanity. The cost will be too much.

A burned bridge can be repaired, although in the physical sense it won't be the same bridge.

With relationships, whether at work with a company and/or coworkers or outside work with friends and/or family, a bridge once burned may take a long time and dedication to rebuilding. It will take effort from all sides to be rebuilt, if it can.

It will take time and trust isn't easy to rebuild. There may be plenty of moments where sincerity is questioned.

Actions will often speak louder than words, as words may be difficult in the early stages. As with many things in life it may take many small steps to get there.

Loyalty is a two-way street between employer and employee. It works only when both manage the relationship. Too often companies expect blind loyalty but do not return the favor.

There are plenty of articles on the web on the subject.

With the mass layoffs of late by many large, rather rich companies, it feeds the narrative that companies don't care.

Let's change that.

Summary

Business cannot expect loyalty, as well as the leadership within, if they are not giving it. Far too often leadership feels that their position and authority give them automatic loyalty. That may be for certain, rare outlier positions in life, but overall, it is not the common mindset by the vast majority of the employees.

You cannot expect people to treat you with respect and provide loyalty when you do not provide the same to them. If you do expect it, you may be delusional in your position and role, especially if you are treating those under your care with disinterest and disregarding their opinions and feelings.

For leaders it is important that they not allow their title and position to go to their head and remember that they too are also human. Titles and positions should not be something lorded over people in a power trip.

Leaders must remember that they too were in the place of those in their employ and treat them as they wish to have been treated in the past, as well as they wish to be treated in the present.

Chapter 13
Toxicity

Toxic seems to be the word of the day. It is a serious issue though as the environment in which we work in day in and day out should be a safe place, free from traits that make up toxic workplaces.

It certainly feels from social media, news and other methods that bombard us daily that leadership within companies certainly feel that their employees do not matter through the actions they are constantly taking against them. It feels the business world has taken a setup to an older age of time where certain practices were permitted.

As a society we should strive to get better, to evolve in a positive direction, not set ourselves back.

Next are thoughts on this divisive topic, in no particular order.

Are you being bullied at work?

No different than when a child in school, it can be frustrating, especially now that you are an adult.

Shouldn't we be better than that as an adult?

Being intimidating, being ignored/isolated, shamed/unduly criticized, impossible expectations put on you, constantly changed requirements, shifting blame to you, intentionally taking credit from you are just some ways you can bullied. It can be emotional, mental and physical attacks.

If a company has a strong culture where no one will tolerate such acts, then there are methods and tools at your disposal.

If not and Leadership and HR allows it, there are not many choices left to you.

All people deserve a safe environment, whether at work or home.

DARVO.

Some will use the DARVO technique when they try to pass off accountability and is often a tool narcissists use to coerce and manipulate those around them.

They will deny, deny, deny.

They will then go on the attack and put the blame on the other person, reversing the roles, becoming the victim I stead of the offender.

This can happen at work, home, anywhere.

It is a form of abuse, whether emotional, physical or mental.

Often you cannot persuade someone using this thought process to change. The only solution is to stay away from them.

That is not an easy solution depending on the situation.

Stay calm and firm in your position. Seek help from others around you when possible and document encounters.

Take care of yourself. No one should be expected to go through such a situation at work, home or elsewhere.

Don't be a manipulator either at work or in your personal life.

Persuasion is one thing, but manipulation is full of negative connotations that can lead to a toxic environment.

It is important to keep insanity out of the workplace. Insanity, not as in clinical, but expecting something new to happen when the process (or a lack of one at times) remains the same.

The cycle needs to end to get new and better results.

Negativity is out there whether in our personal lives or at work. At work it is a drag on a team and company if unhealthy traits are expressed daily and then rewarded.

Arrogance, ego, vanity, self-centeredness while entertaining in a show like Suits, is not conducive to a healthy workplace and life.

If the team accomplished a goal, there is no I in Team. Credit should be given from actions not just talk.

Just my two cents.

No one wants to work in a toxic, hostile, negative workplace day in, day out.

I know speaking for myself, I prefer to keep the drama to tv shows and movies and not in my daily life.

For larger organizations, it may be difficult to keep politics out of the workplace, with various hierarchies/org structures in place. These elements though generally only create a difficult place to spend much of our day. It can cause high turnover and unnecessary stress to the employees and leadership. Valuing the team that supports the business should be the primary goal, not tearing down the team.

It's important that leaders create a workplace free of chaos and distractions that allows employees to thrive in their roles. There can't be a safe, quality environment with uncertainty clouding the workplace

Great leaders set out to make a positive difference/impact in the workplace. Be a great leader.

Ever heard of care washing?

When a company has the facade of a good culture, but turns out differently, once you peel back that facade... that is care washing.

It is an illusion that alienates employees, demotivates them and will likely cause an exodus.

It is important for any business to be transparent and open from the beginning, otherwise they will just waste everyone's time.

Having the right kind of culture, the right kind of perks is important. Frivolous trinkets and perks will not help keep the employees motivated and moving forward for the client/customer, which in turn helps the business.

Lying is far worse for the reputation of any company.

Summary

Toxicity is an overused word these days, but it is because it is so prevalent across the companies millions work in around the world. While employees have been fighting back, as well as some in management, it takes the Sr. Leaders across all companies to start back in the right direction.

Put people first, the people who are making the company successful through their interactions with the customer/client.

Money builds from there, if that is all they care about. Putting finances first will have an opposite effect, even if it takes a while.

The consumer of the business will take notice.

The relationships between the employer and employee will never get better until the executives and leadership make a concerted effort to mend the fences that have been crushed from actions that have alienated so many.

Chapter 14
Finances

Far too often executives and Sr. Leaders only focus on finances, leaving other important elements in the business to dangle in the wind. While money is of course important in order to stay in business, greed and avaricious can detour the vision originally setup for the business. This will often and certainly historically has left the employees and often the customers treated with no regard and tossed aside for short term gains.

That does not help anyone, most certainly the company doing it.

Next are some thoughts on this sensitive subject, in no particular order.

Great leaders don't look solely at money, #'s.

They look out for the team that makes the money, the numbers, which supports the client/customers.

They ensure the team is supported.

They ensure the culture and environment is a positive one.

Focus on the people and everything else will fall in to place.

It seems these days the focus is only the bottom line, and often the bottom line tends to be fine and people are still sacrificed. Greed, avarice, gluttony in the business world needs to end.

People are catching on. The consumers are already moving on from some bigger corporations. Bad decisions, actions, poor planning have consequences.

Top talent will have no interest in working for companies who continually show zero loyalty for employees.

Let's win by working together, planning for a positive future and treating each other with dignity.

Something that doesn't seem to be the case for many companies these days is putting people over profits.

It simply means that employees are valued, which in turn drives sales for services/products.

People are who make profits, who provide excellent services or products for the clients/customers. They are the face of the business and if they are treated well and are happy, that translates into happy clients/customers.

You put profits over people, you will lose your skilled workers and eventually everyone and have no business. Clients/customers will go elsewhere, and we have seen this.

Companies need a profit to stay in business, but it should never happen at the expense of their people.

While it is important for any business to track costs in order to stay in business, coats are not the only element that is important.

It is vital that while the company leadership drives for strong earnings for shareholders, it is equally important to ensure employees are taken care of. Sacrificing any element of social responsibility, environmental responsibility, morality, ethics, quality, safety, transparency and customer requirements will severely backfire.

There needs to be a holistic view within a company on how to be successful.

The workforce will eventually become disengaged, morale will tumble, burnout will occur from stress, turnover will start to become costly, and trust will be nonexistent.

Putting employees first will create an environment where the business will thrive and customers will want the service or product offered.

It feels that in recent years that companies are treating employees as less than human and more as a number. It has always been that way to a certain degree but feels like it has become more prominent of late.

When leadership treats its employees poorly it will trickle down to the customer. This will impact the company's reputation if not handled and the bottom line will eventually go into the negative.

Treating employees as human beings, respecting them and treating them fairly will create a positive environment which will become successful for the customer and their needs.

Seeing billion and trillion dollar (value) companies lay off thousands when earnings didn't quite reach a certain mark, or other reasons doesn't look at the root of the issue and find ways to grow outside of just getting rid of bodies.

While I own stocks and understand the stockholder prospective of making money, this mentality as a sole solution destroys families/lives and also inhibits other parts of the economy.

From a company culture perspective, ensuring a quality product/service is in place & ensuring safety is in mind are all important and will only be cared about by employees who are treated well & with respect.

Summary

Finances in any business is important and should be on the minds of leadership. Finances though should not be all that is on their minds, as it will end up sacrificing the ones who make the money for the company, its employees.

There certainly can be a healthy balance with all involved, as has been the case in the past. As a society we need to move back to what worked for the many, and not what only works for a few.

Chapter 15
Words Matter

There is too much talking these days with little to no actions. What words you use matter when at work. It is important to walk the talk, because if talking is all you do, you will lose those around you through inaction.

Often you will find those who are good at talking are the ones who are elevated into higher positions of authority as they smooth talk their way there. The problem is they sometimes have nothing to back it up. They then rely on those who do the work and act, rather than just talk, to support them.

It is important that those who may be on the quieter side be recognized for the good work they do, instead of focusing on the people who love to hear themselves speak.

Next are some thoughts on this.

Be a doer.

The world has too many who simply talk and certainly there are many out there who just criticize.

Thinking and talking is okay if it is a part of doing something actionable in a timely manner.

For those who tend to criticize, solutions make a difference to most situations. Bring a solution with you. Be part of a solution and not problem.

Often it is thought that to show or be confident you need to be loud and boastful.

That is simply not the case. It is often more the case that when people are loud and boastful, they are insecure.

It is also obnoxious. Those in higher positions will get away with it because of the level of power they have, but respect will probably not be given.

It is often a sign of weakness that others will prey on.

Those that are quiet will often speak when needed and watch and listen in the meantime.

Talk is often cheap with actions being all that matters, which may not occur. Actions take listening and thinking to implement effectively when the time is right.

Don't be deluded to think that you can always talk your way through or out of situation and arrogance and brashness has its limits.

Humility goes a long way to achieving respect from colleagues. If not, they may not be the people to want to be around.

Humor is also important as there are times, we take ourselves and situations too seriously.

The world doesn't revolve around us, even if we think it should at times.

Perception and awareness of ourselves and others is important to remember whether at work or home.

Summary

The words we use everyday matter. How we use them, What words we use, and Who we use them with.

There are many who are good at talking out across the world, which is fine for them. Words alone are empty without actions behind it, especially in the business world. Words will just waste time, especially in meetings. If you do not act on the words spoken, why do it unless you just like to hear your own voice? Some do by the way.

Chapter 16
Solving Problems

Whether a single person, or team, solving problems at work before they become an issue for the customer/client, is a worthwhile action. Problem solving takes some skill, some ability to investigate the little details to get to a bigger problem and overall solution.

There are different ways to solve problems. Different methods, some taking longer than others and more complicated.

From experience, unless the team is made up of extreme experts, the easiest method is the best to use so everyone can be involved.

Next are some thoughts on this, in no particular order.

Whether online or in the real world, people who only bring problems with no solution are of no value. You have a problem, an issue to address, bring a solution with you.

It shouldn't just be on leadership to come up with ideas and solve a problem. Only bringing up problems just leads to being seen as a complainer.
If you bring ideas along with a problem and are ignored, that is another issue.

Online there is what is called a troll, someone who intentionally provokes, criticizes, is negative and attacks continually, often for no apparent reason. Information, and facts provided do not dissuade them.

I would say that trolls are not confined to just the internet.

People, whether they are doing this on purpose or not, have no place in civilized society. They should be blocked by everyone and ostracized.

Free speech doesn't mean freedom from consequences.

Do not feed the trolls. Instead we should work towards a platform, any and all, that no longer supports them in any way.

Additionally, they should not be permitted in the business world to further steer a toxic environment and certainly should not be in our personal lives.

Using the 1-3-1 method at work for problems may help to alleviate issues by breaking them down in a somewhat simple and quick way to solve the problem.

Of course as with most things, it will only be effective if embraced.

Identify the issue and come up with 3 possible solutions and then pick one that will work the best.

This is a way to get a team to work on issues and solutions, not just the leadership... but will only work if allowed to.

One, the employees involved have to take it seriously and not just put crazy and impractical solutions on the table.

Two, leaders need to delegate the ability for employees to practice the 1-3-1 method.

Three, the entire team needs to use it to their benefit. Passing off issues only to leaders and not taking initiative or accountability won't help, and leaders not supporting the team's ideas and initiative will tank the effort.

Methods and processes only work when effort is taken.

It's not my problem is something that will doom a business.

Whether it is Quality related, Safety related or something else, not taking responsibility for key aspects of a business will sink it.

Not understanding your surroundings and the reason why certain things are the way they are will also sink a company. Certain things in the workplace are everyone's responsibility and will only work when the team collaborates.

Whether a company calls it a Quality Circle or by another name as they have evolved over the years, it is important to get engagement in problem solving and improvements. When opinions are taken from employees and not just management, they are a part of decision making and can make a positive impact in what they and their co-workers do. If properly run and maintained, it will make the business more efficient and effective in the long run.

Summary

It is important to identify problems when they are found and get them corrected before they get out of hand.

Whether you are alone to work out issues or with a team, it is important to identify them early, act timely, solve the issue through a thorough review, and implement actions that will fix and prevent the issue from reoccurring.

Controls in place and elimination are just a couple of methods, but it needs to be effective. There are plenty of risks in business. Treating risks with proper attention will keep you out of trouble. Ignoring them or covering them up will only temporarily work, maybe, and will undoubtedly cause further issues down the road.

Even small issues found need to be properly handled before they become bigger issues.

Chapter 17
Flexibility

As a leader, it is important to understand the work and workload your team is handling. It is equally important to ensure there is some flexibility in the workplace for your employees, as issues happen that need to be handled in life outside of work.

While some sectors of work may be more flexible than others, it is on the leader to look after their employees, and includes their health, whether mental, physical, emotional or spiritual.

Business and life evolve over time as elements within change, new generations enter the workforce, and mindsets alter. We all need to be flexible with these ever-changing events.

Next are some thoughts on this, in no particular order.

In this day in age, especially with technology, flexible working hours should be more the norm than the exception.

There are going to be certain fields, especially the service industry that may be more rigid. Unless there is a major shortage of employees in any place, people can certainly use flexibility to handle events in their life from picking and dropping off kids from school and events to going to college to appointments.

It helps morale, and unless productivity slumps, there is no justification to not allow it. Client/Customer requirements will often take precedence but should still be reviewed for applicability.

What kills morale, as well as productivity, is if leadership uses flexible and does now allow their employees to.

Hypocrisy rarely goes over well.

There have been recent studies and experiments with 4-day work weeks that showed more productivity.

If this is an idea to do more work with less people over more time, I question the long-term success and motive behind it. There are also studies out there that show working more hours does not generally produce more or certainly better quality work.

In certain fields, flexibility needs to become the norm for employees.

The mindsets behind some recent corporate moves does not show an effort for a value based work environment that will produce great quality work for customers. Anti-employee policies seem to be a new fad and doesn't seem like a good long-term strategy. Customers also see this and will choose another option when available.

Remote work has been around for a long time. It just became more popular in recent years due to COVID.

Not every company or even section within a company can do it because of a variety of reasons. Not all fields can do it because of the need for customer facing positions or hands on work needed to be accomplished.

Those that can should be permitted to. There is a lot of information on the web that supports the notion that it can work. From experience I know it can.

Not every person will thrive in a remote environment, but that shouldn't mean the majority can't. Also doesn't mean those who are hesitant can't overcome it.

Same goes for leadership. Not every leader has the capability to lead from a distance. That shouldn't mean that employees should pay the price of their leader's incapability. Leadership is about learning, growing and adapting as much as mentoring and leading others.

In this day with costs rising fast and pay not always matching, saving gas money or lunch money could mean paying a bill or not.

Leadership needs to consider this within their organization as an option and not immediately dismiss it due to old mindsets.

The results from the output of work should be the focus, regardless of where you sit.

There is plenty of training out there for leaders, or anyone really, to learn about how to lead and work on remote teams.

Collaboration is still very much possible even when remote. Sometimes more so and often too much with the ability to click on MS Teams or Google Meet or other such tools.

Be a present leader, whether in person or virtual.

Understand that whether in person or virtual, there will always be unique challenges to face and overcome.

Technology will have its ups and downs here and there, but it is here to use and here to stay to some degree. Technology, like all things, will evolve as it has for decades.

Don't throw away an idea of remote work, or even hybrid because of the perceived difficulty. Use it and it may surprise you how it can benefit a team and company.

This has been a hot topic in news for some time with opinions on both sides.

Working remote.

Not every position can be done remote, especially those in-service industries and manufacturing as a couple examples.
But there are plenty that can be. IT related jobs as an example.

Having successfully ran a team remote through trying times and a huge workload, I know it can be successful if done right.

Yes, for new folks on a team, remote can be more challenging. Many like the in-person interactions, but technology allows us to be there for each other through audio and video. Might not always be the same thing but if used correctly will be just as useful.

For leaders who need to know what is going on, KPIs (reports) are a useful tool to use to see the team's output. Communication with the team on status and if they need assistance is important, without delving into the micromanaging realm.

If leadership has no way to know what is going on, they may be negative towards remote work. The time through the COVID 19 pandemic though, showed the world that they can be as or more productive at home than in the office. There are plenty of stats out there on the subject.

Businesses can in many cases save money by re-utilizing their offices for something else or selling it.

You will see a mixed bag from companies and leadership, but there are more stats to find for the positive than the negative regarding the subject.

Are you busy, or productive?

You might have thought that is a misnomer as you night believe they are synonymous with each other. You can be busy and not productive and that probably happens a lot.

Often we can get so busy we forget things, rush and make mistakes and generally fall below expectations of ourselves and possibly others.

It is important to take steps to organize our days and ensure we are setting ourselves up for success.

Efficiency is key.

While maybe not 100% possible in all cases and can be abused by some, flexibility is important for employee's wellbeing & mindset. In the end if their results are positive for the company and customer/client then that should be all that matters.

Summary

A rigid workplace will rarely produce happy or even satisfied employees which in turn will impact the business in a negative manner? How you might ask? Unhappy employees will not be as successful for the customer/client requirements. They will not care about the outcome. They have no interest in providing a great service to the customer/client. They could even sabotage the work.

Leaders need to remember it is the workers, day in and day out, that provide the service or create the products that satisfy the customer/client. Treat the employees right, and they will treat those who buy your services/good in a way that brings them back.

Pretty simple right?

Chapter 18
Feedback, Disagreements & Defensiveness

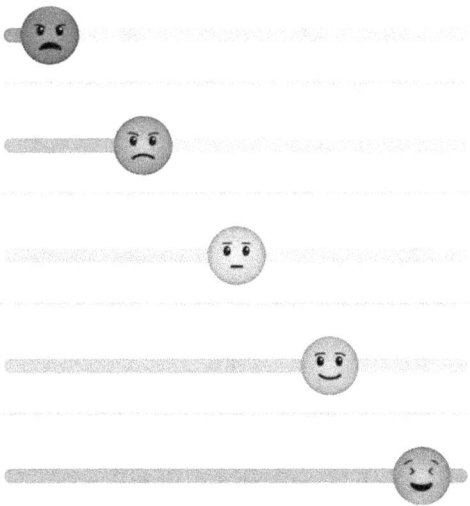

Feedback allows us to know how we are doing, which is critical in our roles at work. Without feedback we are aimless with no direction on how we are doing, which can be frustrating and cause an environment that people will flee from. We may not always accept the feedback and disagree with the assessment but having none can often be worse.

There may be times we get defensive at work, either protecting ourselves, our work or just trying to explain to leadership or a colleague on a task or result. It is rarely pleasant and often the one putting you on the defensive feels attacked and will call out your action. They need to understand, and often properly listen, to avoid this.

Next are some thoughts on this, in no particular order.

Feedback is important in our lives. It should be constructive and actionable.

Vague and unconstructive feedback is simply useless. You won't gain any insight with no useful, concrete information to learn and grow from.

Leadership is meant to help and mentor employees, not hinder or destroy them.

It is easy for employees to get frustrated when they get usually one sided, empty feedback and little to zero information from their leadership.

There are plenty of stats out there on the web that shows employees end up leaving when this does not improve.

If that is the intent by the leadership, that is not the proper way to lead. It will damage the workplace and cost the company in the long term.

It should never be hard to give clear, concise instructions to employees and clear and concise feedback on the results.

Open and clear communication simply makes a stronger workplace which in turn improves the client/customer relationship with motivated and goal driven employees.

In our lives, whether at work or in our personal lives, there will be disagreements.

Disagreements are a part of life and we need to understand that. There is a difference between disagreements and disrespect.

It is important to keep an open mind and listen. Not everyone knows everything about everything, regardless if you think you may. Setting ego aside is generally an important part of coming to an understanding and compromise.

Leadership needs to utilize their employee's expertise and employees need to understand that leadership cannot always move on an idea immediately.

Respect goes both ways in relationships. It cannot be expected from only one party.

We will not always agree with one another, family, friends, colleagues, client/customers, but it is important to not let the difference in opinion lead to disrespect, anger and hatred for one another.

A goal in our lives needs to be to get rid of those toxic behaviors and attitudes from our lives, otherwise life will continue to be unnecessarily difficult.

Over the years I have often heard brought up in discussion the words defensive and combative. Sometimes they are used interchangeable.

Someone may be on the defensive when issues are brought up to them and the one who brings it up feels they are being combative in their defense.

It is rarely ideal when these situations occur at work, but not everything at work is going to be pleasant unfortunately.

Defensiveness is a natural reaction to a situation that is less than ideal. You may not take the criticism as positive or necessary at the moment.

It is equally important for the one providing the critique to not enflame the situation with certain words that may provoke unnecessarily such as assuming the defensive nature is an immediate negative. Words and body language matter for both parties.

A leader jumping right to warning the person of their defensive or combative posture often won't help the situation. The one on the receiving side needs to, although possibly difficult in the circumstance, remain calm.

Throughout our lives we will all learn and grow in our jobs, and that may entail some difficult discussions from time to time. It should be a learning experience for the positive. That is something both parties need to remember sometimes.

Summary

We will not always agree with each other, but feedback is important to ensure we are on track with whatever we may be doing. There are constructive criticism and just hurtful words that help no one.

It is important that to eliminate the need to go on the defense, that leadership and anyone really who puts a colleague into the situation, understands first what they are asking and understands the possible sensitive situation they are in.

That takes a level of emotional intelligence that they may not possess. Emotional intelligence is an important aspect of how we interact with each other. Without it there will be more negative situations surrounding discussions and feedback.

Work on listening first.

Chapter 19
Reports & KPI's

While reports are important to track key performance indicators that each company will have, it is important to not abuse and overuse them. Relying on them alone may miss something because there may be data you are not tracking. Reports can also take some of the human nature out of the workplace through just data and number crunching and not touching on the hands-on work employees are doing for the customer/client.

Data can also be manipulated, so it is important to understand the source to ensure that the report being reviewed gives an accurate picture.

Next are some thoughts on this, in no particular order.

Within any company, reports are used to gauge how a business is running.

Each company, each leader, will want information differently.

Whether on an excel, word based memo or a power point, the data and information presented in charts, graphs or bullet points need to convey what leadership needs to see and know.

Data is meant to be used to empower the leadership team and all employees to focus on what is working and what is still needed to grow.

Reports will always change as circumstances change.

Death by PowerPoint.

I am sure you have heard it and dread it.

It is important that if you have to present using PowerPoint that you don't go overboard with content.

Generally after a half hour you begin to lose people, certainly after an hour.

My general rule of thumb for years has been 1 to 2 minutes per slide max and that gives me an idea how long it may take.

Don't read word for word on the slides. Talking can prolong the presentation as much, if not more, than the number of slides.

Know the slides and touch on highlights. It is often not the slides that are the problem, but those presenting or controlling the meeting.

I find every day there are folks out there that even with an automated tool such as Power Bi, for example, that they still prefer to spend hours playing with excel.

Now excel has been around for over 25 years, so there are a lot out there that is used to it.

For one-time reports, such as an ad- hoc request, it may be okay as it can take many hours or days to develop an automated report. The intent though is to automate and save time reviewing data. A Power Bi report can evolve over time, but it should be useful to the audience.

Creating a report is challenging but reading it shouldn't be. That is where feedback comes into play.

While data manipulation is considered a positive term in data science by arranging information in a way it can be easily read, there can be negatives to manipulating data.

It is important that data is transparent, and the right data is being collected and viewed. Hiding certain data or not even collecting the data through reports can in the long term become detrimental to a business.

Micromanaging is never healthy in any environment. It takes a healthy balance between employers and employees to be successful and not abuse the situation for either party. Its often times forgotten that working in the office will have moments where it appears you may not be working. Talking/shooting the breeze with colleagues, sitting in long meetings not able to multitask, walking around the floor, etc. This is why real KPIs are important to track.

Summary

Reports, lovely reports. While they are often needed for leadership to track results to know what is or is not working, they can be abused.

Technology in some cases has made developing and visually reporting KPI's to leadership and employees alike easier. Technology though requires skill and interest to learn and use. If leadership won't use it, it is useless and makes it more time consuming for the team to develop other, often manual, reports to present.

Use simple methods and lessen wasted time with whatever is needed to stay on target with goals. Don't have pointless reports made. Don't have the team develop something no one will ever view. Keep it simple.

Chapter 20
Technology

The world has become interconnected through technology, and it is changing fast. There is plenty of software and systems out there to use and each company uses something different. It is important that at any level within the company, that you have some ability and knowledge to use them to stay on top of work.

No matter the years and experience you have, there will be learning curves when moving to different companies and even different departments within the same company. One company could have multiple systems to use and it may take time to learn them, which should be understandable.

You would think this to be a logical statement, but many companies expect people to go into a job and ready to use whatever system the company is using. If it is a popular system, understandable, but sometimes it may not be. Some companies have proprietary systems that anyone from the outside will need to learn.

Next are some thoughts on this subject, in no particular order.

Digital Literacy.

It has become a digital world.

As such it is important that in order to both survive and strive to become better, that we learn how to use the digital tools available.

The younger generation has grown up with technology available to them since birth and it is often easier for them. Those of the older generations tend to be slower to adapt. Embracing newer technologies and tools is rare and often it is the 20 to 30 year old tools that are used.

People use what they are comfortable with, but that also stunts growth. Change is not easy when you are used to doing things the same way for years or decades.

With technology the hard part often is creating x, y, z. Using it, depending on the system or tool, is not as complicated.

Having an open mind is the starting point. At work that goes for leadership and employees alike.

While we should look for ways to improve what we do, especially in the business world, we should do it in a balanced manner.

Too often people are treated like numbers, but employees are not robots and need to be treated with dignity.

Looking for efficiencies often are at the cost of people. People cannot be at 100% at all times, especially if working long hours. That is when burnout occurs.

Utilizing machines, AI and technology in general is the way of the future. Like all changes that have occurred since the industrial revolution began well over a century ago, it may change occupations and how we do what we do.

Regardless of that, companies need to remember that it is the people that make connections with customers, and work to make a successful business.

Not handling how improvements are implemented properly and effectively and not ensuring staffing is where the company needs to be, just makes for an uncertain and difficult workplace to be in.

From a Quality standpoint you want people to love Quality and want improvements in the workplace that helps themselves and their customers. If they become tied to negative connotations, then companies and employees within will shun both and the environment will be worse off for it.

Recent events have made for certain sectors of employees to wonder where the future is heading and leaving 10's of thousands or more currently wondering about their futures.

This has occurred in the past but the world has changed since COVID arrived on the scene and the work environment has changed.

It is important now that accountability at all levels in organizations be held to and transparency of business practices be open.

Make people feel recognized, useful and worthwhile. Quality will stay strong; customers will be happy, and businesses will grow.

As seen in the news, especially of late, the idea of technology such as AI or robots taking jobs is on people's minds.

Industry and Quality 4.0 has been out there for a while but has been slow to start. Quality 4.0 is the next revolution in Quality, utilizing technology to make what we do more efficient.

There is still a lot of manual work done, especially with reports, that can currently be automated. Change isn't always easy or accepted and folks like doing whatever they have been comfortable with.

With that said, Lean is about removing wastes in the workplace which this is one. It takes leadership to start implementing new ways to capture data and to make the workplace more efficient, and then it will trickle down.

Let's start.

Some of us may get hundreds of work emails a day on top of our personal emails. It can get overwhelming.

Not everything can be face to face which is why it's important to review your inbox daily. Whether it is email or a Google Meet/MS Teams or other digital forums a lot of the flow of information is digital. Often that is a record of a phone call made earlier or an in-person discussion to refer back to when needed.

It is vital that employees at work, and especially leadership, monitors their digital communications daily to not miss out on vital information. This has also become important in a remote world that a lot work in now.

Don't get left behind in this technological world we live in.

Summary

Technology changes all the time. We have undergone so many changes since the industrial age where jobs that were prevalent are no longer around. With

AI, machine learning and other high-tech tools swooping in and replacing people, we must adapt as we have in the past.

Technology can help us, but it can also be abused. It is on us to regulate that and make it work for us, not against us.

Chapter 21
Meetings

Meetings. The bane of many across the globe. There are so many meetings that simply waste time and are not productive. Just search online and you will find plenty of studies and opinions from many leaders who will agree. Even with that, there are still plenty of unnecessary meetings that could have been an email, message or nothing.

Whether leaders use meetings to exert power over their employees, or just like to hear themselves talk, they need to look at it from an efficiency standpoint and eliminate wasted time and focus instead on what will make them successful for their customer/client.

Next as some further thoughts on this touchy subject, in no particular order.

If a meeting is truly needed, there are some methods to use to manage it and even make it fun.

Just some are:
#1. Plan it well in advance if possible. Give everyone time.
#2. Have the right people involved.
#3. Have an agenda.
#4. Set ground rules for the meeting if needed.
#5. Stay on track and time.
#6. Get feedback.

There are plenty of other tips out there to help improve meetings when they need to occur.

Always utilize emails and chat systems available when possible to avoid a meeting that will take up valuable time for the team.

Keep meetings Lean when possible when they are required.

Meetings.

In the business world they are usually necessary to have to stay on top of situations and tasks. It is important though that if a meeting is truly needed, where an email or memo/SITREP couldn't convey the message, that it stay on time and task.

Unproductive meetings simply waste time and take employees away from tasks. They can also affect morale and drain energy from the team.

Excessive meetings and excessively long meetings can lead to meeting overload. Brain drain, exhaustion and productivity decline will be the result.

Limit to must have meetings, as in only critical. Keep them short & stay on agenda. There are many ways to stay on top of activities without pulling a number of folks away from work.

You'd be surprised what you can do in a day when you break down the time and tasks.

There are times though where what we have on our plate becomes overwhelming. It is important to use tools and methods to help control your time at work and your home life.

You can find plenty of ideas online.

Those responsible for meetings and resources at work hold the key to success in time management for their employees as those elements can be a major hindrance in handling daily tasks.

A leader should not bombard their team with nonsense, such as unnecessary requests and meetings. They should shield them from such things when they are not needed.

Summary

Meetings can be helpful, useful and needed when put together correctly. They can also be energy and time wasters when not. A poor meeting, especially when it could have been an email or message, saps the team's energy away for the rest of the day.
  A meeting should have a true purpose and outcome that everyone should understand. There shouldn't be confusion afterwards because the results then will be subpar, and more time will be wasted following up with questions.
  Let's focus on cutting out time wasting events at work and focus more on customer/client requirements being met and internal company goals reached. The Sr. Leaders and executives will be happy adopting this if they are serious

about their roles, and the customer/client will certainly be happy if more effort is given to them.

Chapter 22
Time Management

Time management is a critical tool to use each day to maintain the workload and balance we all have. Without it, stress will rise, and failures will occur.

This is something that needs practiced and implemented by everyone in a company, not just a select few. Too often, leadership will not respect their employees' time and make it near impossible for them to manage their time by dumping unknown work on them or give them impossible deadlines to meet.

Even the best with time management will not succeed if their leadership puts undue and unnecessary tasks and timetables on them.

Next are some thoughts on time management, in no particular order.

It may be tempted to keep an eye on the clock, hoping to get the day over with at work.

While it may not reduce your stress and instead increase it, it also often wastes time.

It is important that the focus is on the productivity and output, not necessarily the time it takes.

You should want to be productive and gainfully employed while you are working your allotted hours each day. For leaders it is important that employees are tasked with a balanced workload so there are not bottlenecks in the operation.

There may always be outliers, those who abuse the time and those who are overachievers. The latter may not sound bad, but long term it could cause burnout if not managed properly.

Balance in everything is often the goal in life.

We all need some time off. Some may take longer than others to realize this. The more we work without a break, especially with long hours, the less productive and efficient the work will become... even dangerous.

Leadership who doesn't allow a day off will find long term decline in output and high turnover.

It is important to take care of employees as they take care of the client/customer.

We only have 1 life and our health, physical, mental and emotional is important at any age.

There are different ways to work on being productive at work or even in your personal life.

Whichever way you use, as long as you are able to organize your day to become efficient is the goal.

Most of us have a lot going on each day and not having a plan to attack all those tasks and meeting and other events happening, will just cause chaos and stress.

Use the work smarter, not harder mindset every day.

Brain Drain. The term essentially means that you lose your best and brightest to someone else which is rarely good if there isn't someone that can replace them.

There can be several reasons why people leave, but every company, if they are interested in keeping good people as well as their customers/clients, should look into why people are dissatisfied and/or leaving.

In addition, throughout each day there could be a drain on the brain. I've had physical, mental jobs and a combination of the two. Often people will say that mental jobs working behind a desk is easy. Too many meetings, long meetings, unorganized meeting, ad hoc calls, a mountain of tasks can all drain a person each day.

Time and task management needs to be across the board and not just on an employee alone.

Whether in our personal lives or at work there are times we put things off for various reasons.

Whether it's called procrastination or time management, it's important to put focus on what is important in our lives.

Talking about doing something but continuously putting it off means it's either not important, there is an obstacle, or there is a other reason in the back of your mind.

In work we often have those who talk and those who act and sometimes do both. Talking alone won't get the job done. If there is no action, then either drop the idea or plan it with a date for action. If all those involved are not on board it won't be successful.

It can always be brought up later.

How often are you expected to be available 24/7 for a job? Some jobs in emergency services, medical and public works may be in that boat, but even office jobs?

Work-life balance has never been easy or in the past taken seriously, but in recent years it has. Even leaders need to take time off and time away from work to include CEOs. After a long day at work you may want to relax on the couch, take a stroll, go out to eat and not worry about getting a work call. It shouldn't matter if you have family, friends or are single. Your time is precious and should be yours to use as you see fit.

Progress. It won't look the same for everyone. The path taken may be rough at times and may take a while.

Although tempted, you can't really compare your path/journey of progress to someone else's.

No different than giving 100% of your energy and focus on something may actually be 40% one day, 70% and 20% another, it all depends on what's in the tank any given day.

Leaders will often push for something outside the realm of reality and it is important to ensure your team succeeds and not fails with goals.

Summary

It is important that the workplace is grounded in reality, and that includes management of tasks and the time they take. Everyone will handle tasks differently and at different speeds. It is important for leadership to know the difference between fast, slow and those who are having difficulties due to lack of ability.

It is a leader's job is to assist and mentor those having difficulty, and not just toss them aside. It is also their job to put in place reasonable, realistic workloads for the team, and not burn them out.

A workplace will be more productive, and the outcome will meet everyone's needs in the end.

Part 3
Life

Chapter 1
Empathy

It felt while growing up and working a few jobs over the years that empathy was considered weak. This would often impact personal lives. I believe over the years, and especially in recent years, the focus has returned to empathy as an important need and skill in both the workplace and home. I certainly agree with that because as humans, we have emotions that should not be ignored. We have lives with ups and downs that impact us. We need to understand that in order to have productive relationships.

Next are some thoughts on this important topic.

Empathy.

An underrated and often underutilized skill in the workplace.

It is important to understand that we all face challenges each day. Whether at work, home, or elsewhere, we face issues.
Good and bad events occur, but often the bad eclipses the good.

We need to understand that what one person faces will be treated and handled differently than someone else. We each have our limits and it is important to understand that. What one may say is too much, another could say no big deal. Don't brush them aside as sensitive or weak.

This is why empathy is important and underutilized.

Empathy.

While it should be a goal to always do our best at work for the company, client/customer and the team, we are all still human.

Those in leadership positions need to understand that we each have situations in our lives we are facing daily.

That is where empathy comes into play.

Work is just a piece of our lives and it is important that is understood and it is often not. Work, work, work always comes first regardless of how we feel or the situations we are in. That doesn't often work unless there is empathy given for the situation.

Leaders, just like any other employee, are people with situations of their own. A work environment that is open to this understanding will be have better morale, retention, output and will simply function better than a cold, rigid put up and shut up type of workplace.

The environment in which employees work in will often times resonate in the end product or service to the customer/client.

If the proper environment is not there, there is a good chance you won't get what you need out of everyone.

That is why international standards from ISO talk of this and not just from a Quality or Safety standpoint, but in most of their standards.

Building and sustaining a positive, successful environment will get the company culture where it needs to be for the success of the mission.

Empathy and Emotional Intelligence may seem like soft skills, but they should be treated as hard skills. They are fundamental to the well-being of a workforce and in turn production levels that ensure success for the customer/client. Without it the Quality, Safety and Business Culture will suffer.

Summary

Empathy should never mean weakness, as I am sure some across the world feel it is. It is not a weakness to care for your fellow colleagues, friends, family and strangers. Understanding people's feelings, their motivation, their opinion should never be looked down on.

As people, no matter where we are in this world of ours, we should carry with us empathy for living creatures we interact with.

It will make everyone's life easier, better, more fulfilled, and stress, anxiety and the evils around us would begin to vanish.

It may be idealistic, but the more that employ it, the more standard it will become.

Chapter 2
A Gift to Yourself and Others

There are things we can do every day that doesn't cost any money, both for ourselves and others.

There are small gifts we can give to others, as small as a smile, a hello, a nod, a helping hand. While doing the opposite is also free, it is of no value. Just because something is free does not mean there is no value. Value of course is in the eye of the beholder, but we should be doing what makes us and those around us better, not worse.

We need to start bringing positive value into our lives, and those around us.

Next are some thoughts to think about, in no particular order.

Each day is a gift. Even when times are difficult and we feel down and desperate, we are still here and able to make the best of what we can for ourselves and those around us.

The "gift" may not be what we expected, but it is a gift nonetheless.

It is important to live in the present and not allow possible future events that may never occur to bring us down.

Some out there may not like inspirational posts, but many do, because it may be just what you need at that moment.

If you impact even one person a day in a positive way through words or actions, you have changed the world for the better.

It is important to understand that we each have this one life. We do not know how long we have.

With that said we should be using it to live. Too often, especially in this modern world, our lives revolve around work.

While I am sure there are plenty out there who have jobs they love, that drive them to go in and give their best each day, we should be working to live and not living to work.

How many people do you know or have known who wished they had worked more and harder when they are on their deathbed? I doubt too many. They wish they had more time to travel, to spend with family and friends, to do something new or different.

Let's not waste our lives. Money is needed to live, yes, but it shouldn't be the only driver.

Just a reminder to find time to enjoy life in some way. While work itself is fine, it shouldn't be the 'be all end all' consuming force in your life.

It only takes a moment, a smile, one small act to change or even save a person's life in a positive way. With everything going on in the world we need more positive change happening.

Our lives are like a candle.

Like a candle, we burn brightly for a time; as the candle wax melts, we grow older. We need to use that light to help those in the dark. Use our knowledge and experience to educate and not to tear down.

We don't know how long before our flame goes out, but we should live every day to its fullest and impact those around us in a positive manner.

The world would be a better place if more did this.

Whether in your personal life or at work, you don't always know what is going on in others' lives. Be there to support, not break down.
We can all find ourselves in a bad place from time to time so help when you can because you may need it in return one day.

Surround yourself at work and in your personal life with those who will support you, encourage you and elevate you for success.

Summary

We each have the ability to make a positive change not just in our lives, but for others, through our actions. Let us all act in a positive way to bring light to the world of darkness.

It may sound easy, but it is not seen around the world each day and through time long past. It takes a concerted effort by everyone to do what is right. Let's do it together.

Chapter 3
Boundaries

Boundaries have historically been frowned upon in life, but are necessary for your health, whether mental, physical, emotional or spiritual.

In a high-tech world, fast paced, money, money. money first work life many are in daily, balance and boundaries are extremely challenging to find.

This is very unhealthy, and the newest generations are looking at what their parents have suffered through and how it affected them. They say no, and I for one am proud of the stand they have taken, often at the expense of their career. The older generations, of which I am a part of, is still often stuck in the old school mentality of work first, fun later, if at all. Some of my generation, the older they have gotten and farther along the rat race, have begun to push back against this mindset as they have finally realized how unhealthy it is. Now we just need more to realize it.

Next are thoughts on boundaries, in no particular order.

The only people who get upset about you setting boundaries are the ones who were/are benefiting from you having none.

Vacations are often described as recharging.

Often vacations tend to be exhausting as we try to cram as much into it as possible.

Need a vacation from the vacation as the saying goes.

We shouldn't think of a vacation as something needed to recharge from work because that means work is burning us out. It may be but that is really the wrong mind set.

A vacation is a chance to get away, even if local, to do something, to see something. Could be new or something not done in a while.

It is an opportunity to be free for a moment to live your life away from certain stresses.

The United States is the only industrial country without federally mandated personal time off. Much of the rest of the world has something in place. This shows its importance in our lives as we only get one and time flies by before you know it.

Leadership should never guilt employees who want to take time off.

Whether it is a personal day, vacation, holiday, shouldn't matter; employees have the right to time away from work.

Leadership can take time off as well, they just often choose not too for whatever reason they have at the moment.

Unless you are an entrepreneur and a small business, most of the time the company will be fine if you are out 1 day, 3 days, a week or a month.

You need that time to relax and declutter your brain.

Life is short. Take the time while you can and not at the end of 50/60+ years of work when you may not be able to any longer.

Live.

Boundaries.

They are important in all aspects of our lives.

There are physical, mental and emotional boundaries to think of.

It is important to know your limits and communicate them.

Although leadership may not always like to hear it, the word no is important to use, even for themselves.

We aren't always able to do x, y, and z or in a certain time frame.

Having boundaries sets expectations, sets what is important and able to get done for employees and management alike.

It helps lower a stressful environment.

It sets up a balance between home life and work. It creates an understanding that we each have varying types of lives.

Just because you like to work on time off or have no hobbies to consume your time, even to just rest, doesn't mean others around you have that same mindset and life.

Management and employees alike need to take some time to understand those around them in order to work better as a team.

There will be people who will disagree and those of us who wish to have proper boundaries who will politely push back against the negative.

Respect is earned but important between colleagues. Setting boundaries begins to earn respect. Respect of one's time, ability, choices.

If the environment does not allow for proper boundaries after clearly communicating the need, then leadership from top down is not interested in instilling it. It may not be the right place to be for you.

Summary

It is important to set boundaries in life. Without it we will succumb to stress, mental breakdown, anxiety, ailments, failed relationships, no relationships, loneliness, and an overall unhappy life. We only get one. Learn to live in the present and enjoy the small moment.

Work never ends in the workplace. Emails never stop. Turn it off and enjoy your off time, no matter your position in life. You, those close to you, and around you will thank you for it.

Don't live with regret later in life.

Chapter 4
Time, Time to Unplug & Value

Time is finite. We only get so much. What we do with it is incredibly important.

While we all with have down days, we should look at our time to ensure we are using it properly and not wasting it. You would be surprised when you look at what you do each day at what you could be doing instead.

I have brought this topic up before and people respond that they just don't have the time to take classes, to learn something new, to do something they haven't done before. Baloney. You want to do it, you will. You can set aside some time each day before or after work, or your off day to read, learn, write, play, exercise or whatever you wish to do. Even if it is only an hour, you will over time achieve success in your goal.

Value is often in the eye of the beholder. What one person values, another may not. There are so many aspects to our lives that have value, whether at work, our personal lives and elsewhere, but which is of more value? This is something we each must determine and treat individually.

Whatever it is that you value, treat it well. Although it may be an individual matter, what you value should be of substance, something that truly matters, that isn't going to hurt, damage or affect those around you in a negative way.

Money as an example is valued by many, but it should be a resource to help you through life, not control you through life.

Time itself is valuable, so treat it well.

Next are some thoughts on time.

What do you do all day?

It is something to think about. We get 24 hours a day. What do we do with it?

Often we tell ourselves and others we don't have time to do x, y, z. Do we?

It is important that if you want to do something, you set aside time to do it.

I had goals set for 2024 and so I set aside time each day to make my goals come to fruition, and they will. I plan on continuing it into the next year.

Even if you work long hours and are tired, if you are serious about it, and have a passion for whatever it may be, you will find the time.

What is important for you to spend time on each day? Use those 24 hours given to you and use them to your advantage and wisely.

Don't live with regret. Time is finite.

There are times it is important to be bored.

We live in a world with so much at our fingertips, it is hard to imagine an opportunity to be bored.

Boredom offers a chance to dwell on our own thoughts, a chance to be creative. This is the time ideas might pop into your brain to write down, or an chance to be creative through other arts.

There are times you just need to have some peace away from social media, electronics, modern society that makes us feel we always have to be plugged in.

Whatever happened to that imagination you once had as a child?

Unplug.

As we grow older, and time passes, we lose many of the traits we had when we were children.

But there are traits of children that we should strive to retain as we grow older. It will make both our personal lives and work lives better.

Retaining curiosity & wonder in life will open us to new looking at ideas and having innovative thoughts. Children are often happy for no reason and that is something adults would benefit from.

Taking some time to look for our inner child may help us grow and become happier even in difficult times. Not necessarily easy, but something to strive for.

What do you value?

Value means different things to different people and companies.

Values can also change over time. As we grow older what we value will change as we learn and grow wiser.

Certain basic values will often remain for most but certain elements within our lives will become less important as circumstances change.

What do you value and how does it drive your life?

There are numerous types of value out there and dependent on the customers need, the perceived value will be different.

The goal is to have a perceived value by the customer in what you are providing. It should be of value.

We should want to provide a Quality service or product. That requires proactivity, value add actions, and a motivated & knowledgeable group of employees who make it work.

We should want to be a value to our client/customer. Internally as a company, employees should also feel valued as that will permeate into what they do externally.

Everyone wants to feel valued at work. The more value you feel, often is tied to better output and alignment with what the client/customer wants.

Having your voice heard and acknowledged as well as your work appreciated goes a long way.

Although we may not think we do, we use Cost Benefit Analysis all the time in our lives. It isn't just for work with new projects or improvement ideas.

Any time you think about getting a new phone or vehicle or even coffee, in the back of your mind (or even openly like myself) you are thinking, is this worth the price? Can I do or get better?

Summary

Time is something we get little of and it is important to use it wisely. Use it to your advantage, not squander it. It is what you make of it. Make it worthwhile.

What do you value? Whatever it may be, treat it well, but keep it in context.
Whether it is a person, animal, possession (s), travel, health, or something else, you have so much time in your life, so treat value as an important commodity.

We all get 24 hours a day to use. How do you use it?

Chapter 5
Frustration & Stress

We all get frustrated and stressed out.

Life can get crazy, both at work and home. How we handle frustration and stress is important. It is easy to become consumed by it, leading to poor decisions that can be rash and cause long term damage in our lives.

We should never allow those around us to put us in that position. We cannot control others, but we can control how we react to situations and in the end, the outcome.

There may be times we must walk away from a situation to take ourselves out of the situation and equation, to breath, to think, before proceeding.

Next are some thoughts on this, in no particular order.

How do you handle stress?

There is stress that will strengthen you and stress that will damage you.

Stress may occur when it doesn't even need to which will make handling it even more challenging.

There are times people come into our lives to test us, for good and bad. And although we may not want it, it will often give us the knowledge, the experience and the strength the endure the future.

The best way to handle stress is to plan for it whenever possible, which is not always an option. A strategy and steps to break down the task or situation will help to ease some of the stress overwhelming you.

Ask for help when needed. Know your limits. Communicate it.

Stay calm and breathe.

Frustration.

We all get frustrated from time to time and it is usually considered a big emotion. It may very well be if it is constant as it can lead to stress.

I saw a post elsewhere that talked about frustration actually being a good emotion to have at times.

Frustration will show that you still care about something.

It will also spur change sometimes.

It will show you what not to do but also what you need to do better or at least work on.

Just don't let it get the better of you.

Stress.

It is something we all live with.

Some is good, much of stress is negative, especially long term.

Each of us have our own limits and only we know them.

Often we will be surprised by how much we can take.

We have to do our best to manage it. At work it can be difficult with growing workloads, last minute tasks and requests, difficult people.

Even though challenging and sometimes difficult, we must find ways to cope and release the stress so that it does not impact us negatively.

It may require a change in our life.

I was surprised when I came across this.

To recover from burnout could take years. A day off or a vacation won't help long term.

It is important, whether in our personal lives or in a work environment, to admit there may be a problem. Then you can work towards the goal of getting better.

This is as important for a business as it is to an individual. It may take a while, but the first step is acknowledging a problem, then seeking assistance and sticking with a plan of action.

It's difficult to always be at 100%.

Even the best out there has bad or odd days.

Constantly being expected to be at 100% or higher will eventually lead to burn out or worse. It may take a month, year or decade but our minds and bodies will eventually give out.

While high performance at work may not always be there 100% of the time, we should still strive to do our best. Reach out to those around you if you need help and together goals can be achieved.

Are you feeling burned out at work? Stress can be a positive at times, but too much for too long will wear you down.
Whether at work or in our personal lives, burnout can happen.

Always reach out to those around you, if you can, as talking can often times release some of the tension.

How do you handle it?

Work Life balance is important and there are a lot of studies and information you can get on the web on the subject. You need to be able to step away from work and not just a vacation. Unless you are on call for a specific reason, taking time to relax is key to mental health. We after all are not robots.

Summary

It isn't easy to say no, and sometimes it can be dangerous depending on your boss, or family and friend you are saying no to. It is also important to understand and learn when to say no.

When you are younger, especially at work, you want to succeed so you will go the extra mile to get to that position you want in life. As you get older, that may not be as important. You realize the older you get, the less time you have to achieve what you really want in life, what you really want to do. Choose wisely. Ask those around you who have gotten that far for advice, because as you age and experience, you learn.

The younger generation may not always have respect for those older, but if they are willing, they can teach a lot.

Choose those to provide that advice wisely as well because there will be a wide variety across the spectrum who will give good, mediocre, and bad advice.

Look not just at success, but how they succeeded and how they positively impacted those who took their advice. People change and evolve over their lifetime. Advice they gave when they were younger may not be the same twenty years later.

Chapter 6
Perception & Fear

Whether we want to admit it or not, there is something we all fear in life. How we handle that fear will determine how we live with it because fear should not rule our lives. That may not be easy dependent on the fear.

What we perceive around us may not be what is happening. We may think people have an opinion of us, good or bad, that may be the opposite of what we think, which may feed our fear or how we act around people. People have a lot going on in their lives, as we all do. There may be issues now, but that will fade as other issues arise in their lives and take their place.

Keep things in perspective.

Next are thoughts on perception and fear, in no particular order.

Don't let others perception of you run your life.

As much as we may want to give off good impressions and want people to like us and respect us, that simply will not happen 100% of the time.

Do not let that desire, and often fear, railroad your life and cause you anxiety and stress. It isn't worth it and often times what we think people's opinions are is not the fact.

Press on and keep doing your best each day in life. Your actions and beliefs are under your control.

Barriers/obstacles in life are meant to go around and not stop you.

What is keeping you from advancing/changing to being what you would consider successful?

What is your roadblock? Is it fear of the unknown? Fear of failure? Self-esteem, lack of confidence? Outside entities not being supportive? No support structures? It is important to have support in your goals.

Your mindset and attitude will determine if you succeed or not as the first hurdle.

Does your company provide support, training, growth and other avenues to learn and grow? If not, you may need to control your own destiny.

Uncertainty is another hurdle. Are you certain you want to go down this path? With economic issues being faced by so many, do you want to take a chance on a change?

Fear is ultimately the biggest hurdle most of us face. Fear of failure and change which leads to the unknown. Fear of trying and failing in your goals and ambitions.

If you want a positive change in your life, to do something, to meet a goal, don't let uncertainty and fear drive away your ambitions. You may regret the decision to not try and you don't want to look back on life with regret.

Fear.

It is a word rarely looked upon as a good thing.

There are leaders and companies who use fear as a tactic that they think will motivate employees to do better.

Wrong. It demotivates employees and puts a high amount of unnecessary stress on them.

Work is a part of life, got it.

Work is what supports our lifestyle, it should not dictate or control it.
It does far too often.

While the world's current use of capitalism has picked up so many millions out of poverty across the word, companies also use it to take advantage of employees. Taking the last drop of energy from them each day. Expecting more and more with less.

When do we enjoy life? There can be a balance.

If fear is continued in the workplace, employees will take that and transfer it to the client/customer. If employees are treated in that manner, the company doesn't really care about their client/customer. While companies may treat their employees as disposable, we can treat companies the same as well.

It is not easy to post something on social media, or to make a tutorial video, or to write a book because when you do all these things, you are opening yourself up to ridicule. That is something most people don't want to do, and it is understandable. You are in a vulnerable state, but you may regret not doing it.

You may have something such as advice that can help someone. Even if one person has a positive experience, that is one person you helped. That is powerful.

Putting yourself out there isn't easy.

You may be apprehensive to put ideas and comments out there for people to critique. Not every post will hit home, but if you impact even one person in a positive way, it is a win.

I have seen some complain they don't get x amount of views or likes, but just think for a minute. Strangers are taking time out of their day to read or view your post. Be grateful.

There will always be trolls out there and nothing you say will dissuade them. Ignore the haters, take advice from credible/valuable feedback and try.

We can always learn from each other. It is a big planet even if it feels small sometimes. There are plenty of great ideas out there to learn from.

Summary

Fear and perception are two elements that are difficult for us to face each day, but we can. We will face both in different ways. There are so many fears out there and so many ways we can perceptive events, people, situations.

It can feel overwhelming.

Reach out to those around you for assistance, advice, help. Sometimes a stranger can help better than those closest to us.

Chapter 7
Learning

Learning never ends. It should not matter how old you may be, because learning keeps the mind young, so it is important to use it.

Additionally, it is important to teach those subjects you may know to pass along knowledge to those who can continue the learning-teaching cycle.

Reading and learning will take time of course, but you can prioritize an hour or less a day and you will learn a subject in no time.

While reading is fundamental, it is neglected in this day in age with videos and technology taking its place. While people learn in different methods, reading, seeing, listening and doing, it is important to do it.

Next are thoughts on this important topic, in no particular order.

While educating and training people on a variety of topics is important and often necessary, putting them into play is what really matters.

Training, reading, listening to an instructor, coach, teacher is great but you need to use it, otherwise what is the point of learning it.

Everyone learns in different ways and sometimes the best way for them is not always available.

But from experience, hand on tends to be the best way to get a grasp on something.

Practice makes perfect and practical application will get you hands on training and knowledge that will make it easier over time. This is often important after the initial training.

It may take time to get a firm understanding and not everyone will get it. Depending on the subject, task, job, not everyone may be capable of doing it as we each have our capabilities. Teams are often made up of diverse groups that feed off each other and complement one another.

While it is great when everyone can do everything the same way, that is not reality and needs to be understood.

Leaders need to leverage the teams capability in the best way for the success of the business for their customer.

We all will normally work at multiple places in our lifetime.

At each we will probably learn something and as we do we may bring those best practices with us.

As we climb the ladder and get into leadership roles, we may want to implement some of those best practices.

When we go to a new company, it is important that we learn about the company and get familiar with it before implementing something.

It is important to not take away best practices that got that company or program/project where it is. It is also important to not implement something that did not work elsewhere or at least didn't help the previous company succeed.

Learning from the past will help ensure that both the negative and positives are known and the future will be positive.

While change happens and is sometimes needed to keep on a positive trajectory, change for the sake of change isn't necessarily needed.

A new leader, especially, tends to want to make an impact. It should be a positive impact, not destructive or negative for the employees who make the magic work for the client/customer.

Leaders often have as much to learn from employees as they must learn from the leader.

Be willing to learn. If you aren't, teaching anything will fall on deaf ears and will not be retained. It won't be beneficial for either party.

We should all want to learn something new as we go through life.

The older we get, the more important it is to stay active mentally as well as physically.

The choice is yours.

In today's world there no longer seems to be the chance to make an argument or discussion without facing retribution.

Intelligent people can discuss a topic, and both be right.

They can also agree to disagree. From the time we are children to the time we are adults we will have opinions. Will we have the freedom to voice those opinions? The more we discuss, the more we learn. Never stop learning.

Reading, Listening, Understanding and Asking Questions are important elements in our lives.

Whether it is reading an email, or taking time to read training material or take provided classes, it is important to read/listen and then ask questions if there are any.

Some don't do either.

It is important at work to understand a task. Communication goes both ways, the sender and the one receiving. If one or the other... or both are not clear, lines will get crossed.

Productivity and time is wasted when this occurs.

Sometimes you just must go back to the fundamentals and work on them like you did in school. Reading, Writing and Listening.

It is important to be willing to learn.

I know I don't know everything and I am always finding ways to learn about a wide variety of subjects, not just in my own field.

As Henry Ford said: "Anyone who stops learning is old, whether at 20 or 80. Anyone who keeps learning stays young."

Training is important in a workplace.

If training is not available there is a good chance that the service/product being provided will be subpar for the customer.

It starts from onboarding, to on the job, to more over the course of time.

Each company will have its own unique training.

In recent years, especially with COVID 19, training moved to an online, virtual setting. Dependent on the size, scale and scope of a company, this may be the norm as it's easier to get people involved at multiple locations. It can save time and money as travel time can add up for in person training.

The majority of people are visual, while the remaining prefers auditory. Only a sliver is hands on.

Now just like with customer service it is important for those being trained understands the other side. Not every company will have a dedicated team and it may be a secondary task.

In most cases constructive criticism is welcome to better the training provided. Unconstructive/destructive criticism is simply a negative situation that doesn't help anyone.

It is important to remember that no matter where we reach on the ladder at work, we all generally started at the bottom somewhere.

Often times that is forgotten when working with others. Ego may get in the way. As leaders we should remember that we were there once and help guide and mentor others to be where they will climb the ladder as well. It shouldn't be a competition but a journey of teamwork.

We all have something to learn from each other.

It's important as a leader to let your team shine. Don't overshadow them. They may have more experience and knowledge then you and that is alright. Either they were hired for that experience and knowledge or you came in to lead a existing experienced team. Let them do what they do and learn what you do not know.

There is often too much ego and title loving in companies when it should be more about the team.

Always be willing to learn.

It is important to never stop learning even as we get older and been working for a long time or in a position for many years.

Even if we strive for no errors, mistakes occur but it is important to learn from them. Make them teaching moments.

Be open and humble with each other. Ego and arrogance tend to drives folks away. Titles are temporary. How we treat each other will be long remembered.

Less ignorance and lack of knowledge will not just make a company better but everyone within better for the future.

We have so much information at our fingertips in this day and age for anything otherwise.

Whether in the business world or in our personal lives, we will come across those not understanding a variety of topics. Education is a pathway to lead to understanding and elimination of ignorance on a topic.

Those who are not interested in understanding a topic, especially work related, goes down another path.

That is separate from having a difference of opinion.

Training is an important piece of being successful at work, but it is only the first step.

Having a can/want to and not and will/won't do is also important.

You can be trained but if you don't want to be there or don't pay attention it is a wasted effort by the trainer and yourself.

Training is a two-way street. Having the right people involved goes a long way to be successful.

Lead by example.

Never stop learning and be open to new and different ideas. Collaborate and Empower your team.

Reading is fundamental.

Whether it is because it is too much to read, not enough time, laziness, procrastination, disinterest, whatever the reason, reading is not being used like it used to be.

With technology in place, the quick fix is what many expect these days.

Especially at work, it is vital to read any written policy and procedure in place to understand the process.

Next comes understanding and if questions are needed, ask.

If there is something out there available to include emails and other communications being used, and everything is ignored, the outcome will rarely be good.

It is also frustrating to the ones who communicate matters because they are being ignored and then their time is being wasted with inquiries asking about something they already sent out.

Reading is fundamental.

It is important to keep learning within our craft and outside it. We can always do with a refresher course every now and then, both as leaders and everyone in general. It also doesn't hurt to dabble in something new every now and then to simply learn about something different.

Embracing self-development is not only good for leadership but also will often get others around them interested in learning, and in turn, growing.

As we get older we may think we have learned it all, done it all, but that is rarely true. Keeping the mind active for as long as possible also helps keep us healthy for longer.

There is so much out there to learn about, and just a little time each day will get you in the right direction.

We all have positives and negatives in our life, whether at work or in our personal lives.

We learn from both. Often at the time a negative situation is seen as such, but down the road a bit you look back and see it was actually a positive.

Often times we need that negative situation to move us past it and into a better situation. That negative turned into a positive. It has happened to me and it happens throughout our lives.

If you are in that type of situation now, use it to your advantage. It is often a motivator to move on, to change, to grow, to move beyond where you are that may be holding you back or hurting you.

We often think of people in our past or even current life that was or is such a negative influence but they are often the reason we may move into a better place, so in a way they were a positive catalyst in our lives.

Don't lose hope. It will get better.

We all started somewhere doing something.

We were beginners, rookies at our job or hobby.

Over time as we continue to work at our job or hobby we continue to get better.

One day after a number of years we may even become experts.

It takes time and no one at the beginning should be afraid to ask questions and their leadership should understand that.

Leaders mentor so the next group of people will become experts.

Experts though should refresh their knowledge from time to time and also learn something new from time to time.

There is always something to learn.

Experience alone, just like training alone, does not mean you have learned to do x, y, z.

We all experience things differently. We each learn from training/coaching differently.

In the end what is important is the evaluation of experience and training to ensure it was processed correctly.

If not, both may lead to different outcomes than expected.

Summary

Learn, learn, learn. Read, read, read. Listen, listen, listen. Doing so will enrich your life, but you must make it a priority.

Put down the phone, set aside the internet, tv, movies, to focus on something that can benefit you.

You'd be surprised how much you can do and learn if you focus and set aside some time. Do it. You will not regret it.

Chapter 8
Making Everyone Happy / Treating People Well

A challenge in life is making those around us, whether at work or home, happy. In doing that, someone will often be left out as experience will show, it is impossible to make everyone in your life happy.

The challenge is to pick your battles and ensure that the right people are the focus. When you try to make everyone happy, you will either make no one happy or only some happy and certainly you will not be happy after the effort.

While making everyone happy may often be out of reach, treating people well is not. No matter our position in life, we should treat all those around us in a humane manner. You may be surprised when you may need help yourself.

We are all in different stages in life. We may go at a higher level now while those around us are in more difficult times, but roles can be reversed quickly. It is also important to remember that as we go through life there are those who help us reach a higher level and we must not forget that.

Next are some thoughts on this difficult situation, in no particular order.

Remember that no matter what we do in life we will not please everyone.

What we do, say, or write may be loved by a majority but hated by others.

There is nothing we can do about it. If you try to please everyone, you will end up pleasing no one and simply stressing yourself out.

Don't stress it.

Learn and grow from objective, useful opinions from people close to you, as well as failures and wins.

Ignore the haters.

Keep moving forward.

We are all human beings. While there are some professions and positions that elicit more expected respect and certain etiquette than others, we should all understand that we are all people.

I have always believed that whether you are the janitor or the CEO, you should be treated the same, fair and humanly.

We are all at varying aspects/levels of our lives, our careers and while you may be on top now, that may not be the case for long.

If you allow ego and title/position to influence how you treat people, especially for the worse, you shouldn't be in that position. You should be able to be spoken with as a human regardless of position and title.

If folks are afraid to give you an opinion, or facts on a situation, something needs to be reevaluated if it is because of how, they perceive you will respond.

Just my thoughts.

Is there a difference between a nice person and a good person?

They are often seen as the same, but there are some differences.

Often being nice may simply mean being polite, not causing waves and seeking approval from those around them, especially leadership.

Being good embodies deeper virtues that we should strive for such as having integrity and working toward making a positive impact on those around us daily.

Often being nice will be seen as a push over while being good looks to take responsibility for actions and activities they are involved in and ensure they hold to positive principles. It may mean holding up the ideal of justice and simply what is right, whether at work or in personal life. That can sometimes take sacrifices.

Treat those around you with decency, no matter what their position in life. Work or in your personal life, it shouldn't matter.

We are all going through something each day.

Acts, good and bad, can have a lasting effect. Titles, in many cases, are temporary and have no lasting impact. What we do while we have them is what matters.

Regardless of the industry and position you are currently working in; whether it is Quality, Safety, HR, IT, Property, Supply, Contracts, Finance and more in either Manufacturing or Services, you should be treated well as anyone else should.

Treat people how you wish to be treated falls on deaf ears until it affects you. When people are treated well, the business will succeed, and our personal lives will become more enriched.

Focusing on Quality especially when everyone is involved, whether in the workplace or life in general, will provide what is expected effectively and efficiently making everyone's life a little bit better.

Summary

Every day we should do our utmost to be civil with one another. We will face people we do not like, can stand or even hate, but we must remain civilized, especially at work, school, or in public.

Relationships will sour, but you still must be around them for various reasons. Not an easy situation, but one where you need to remain calm.

There may be times where the situation has become so hostile that you must remove yourself from the equation. In the end you must do what is best for you and those you love.

Chapter 9
Jumping to Conclusions & Personal Issues

There will be times in our life that without all the information at hand, we jump to an opinion or conclusion that may be wrong. It may not be easiest to do but waiting for all the information may save a lot of heartache, because jumping to a blind conclusion could certainly hurt relationships.

Regardless if at work, home, or public, deciding without facts can have long term implications. Regret should not be something you need to worry about in life, but we often do.

Slow down, don't let your mind race wildly, and use some critical thinking skills. You will save yourself in the long run.

While personal issues tend to be frowned upon at work, they happen. Life happens. Work is just a part of life, not all of it. This is something many leaders do not seem to understand.

It is important that you focus on those issues to fix them and not allow them to fester and get worse. Spend time away from work with yourself, others like friends and family. Focus on your health, your education and knowledge and certainly your passions.

Next are some thoughts on this subject, in no particular order.

Jumping to conclusions is some extra exercise for those who like it.

All it does is cause conflict, confusion and misunderstand. None of these are good and rarely needed.

There are plenty of these types of extra exercises that are not beneficial so stick with the traditional exercises.

And stick with facts as facts are the best to go by when making decisions. Best alternate many times when possible is simply ignore the scenario instead of assuming.

On the flip side of the coin, there may be situations people put themselves into that open themselves to these types of exercises from others. Stay clear of that.

There are times when issues creep up, whether at work, or in our personal lives.

Ignoring those issues can have a detrimental effect on ourselves, our colleagues, friends and family.

We can lose employee morale, team cohesiveness, Client/Customers business if issues are ignored by sweeping under the rug or not being handled timely and effectively.

It is important to get into a proactive state instead of running around constantly putting out fires.

Working openly and diligently with everyone involved will get the issues solved the right way and keep morale up. Ignoring concerns or not involving people will only set things back in the workplace.

Think fire prevention and not firefighting.

Although at times it may be difficult, especially during challenging situations and down times, be thankful for what you do have. Help those around you when you can and find those moments of happiness and joy in life.

It is important to remember that everyone has different levels of threshold tolerance regarding stress and pain.

We can't treat everyone equal in this. It is often case by case at work and our personal lives.

A blanket statement or action will leave someone out and frustrated further.

Everyone goes through something negative at some point in their lives, often many times over the span of a lifetime.

It is important to understand that and understand that people are not robots.

I always heard the saying to leave your home life at the door, but for most people we cannot divorce our personal life from our work life. It is not that easy. To say that it is, is a serious lack of empathy.

Treating people kindly is free in life. You never know what each person you meet is going through. Being kind to a person could make their day.

There are times where the way we think alone could cause us to fail, never mind outside influences.

It's important to understand why we may be thinking the way we are and find solutions to remove it from our lives. It is rarely easy and will require time and sometimes even a new environment.

Jealousy and envy are more negatives that at times permeate our lives. We all succeed at life, whether our personal or professional lives differently and at different times. Don't let others' positions or stature in life deter you from achieving your own.

Certainly, don't allow your work life or home life sour because of what others have that you may not have now. Your time will come if you work for it.

Summary

We will always have personal issues in life. It is how we face them that matters. How we will be judged in life is how we face them.

As with all problems, reach out to those around you for support and don't worry about the negative traits that may exude from some people when you are having difficult times. Not everyone will understand and show compassion and empathy. Brush it aside and seek help from those who truly care, who will listen and help.

It will be okay. Even in the darkest of times we can find the smallest shred of light to guide us back. May be difficult, may seem impossible, you may not feel like it, but letting it guide you will bring you back.

Chapter 10
Honesty

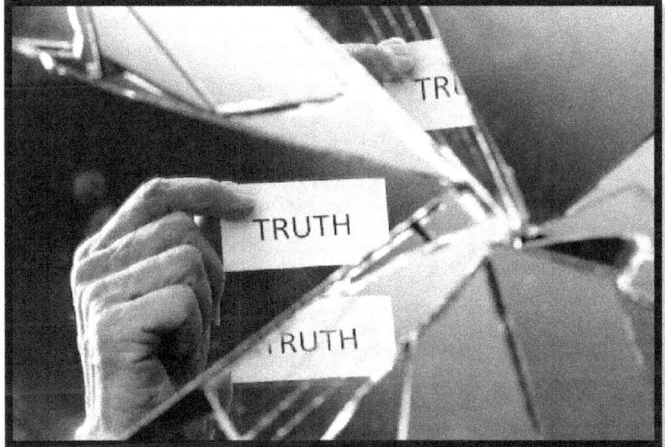

I would hope that most people across the world believe in honesty. It feels though that we are surrounded by dishonest people, whether at work where people are in it for themselves and covering for themselves, at school with people who may not know better, at home to protect themselves from punishment or in public among strangers who don't care about each other.

Honesty, integrity, transparency, accountability, all go together to make someone to become, to want to be around and someone who will be looked upon in awe, wonder and respect, even if it is not always verbalized.

How do you wish others to treat you? How do you treat others? How do you handle situations that are challenging?

What we do, what we decide on, how we handle the truth will define us to others, for better or worse dependent on the outcome.

Next are some thoughts on honesty, in no particular order.

What is the difference between honesty, rudeness and outright lie?

There is often a fine line between honestly and rudeness. There isn't one with a lie.

We should all want honesty. Honesty though should come from a positive side of wanting to help and be constructive. Rudeness is generally negative of course and may not be helpful to the person.

It could be construed as rude by the receiver even if it is not meant that way. It is on ourselves to perceive what we will, positive and negative.

Tone and attitude also plays a part in how we come across as well as how we receive a critique or thought from someone. Unless purposeful for some reason, we should not want to come across as rude.

A lie is flat out wrong the vast majority of the time and unhelpful.

A person's character in the end is what is important in life. Results are one thing, but without integrity, compassion, responsibility, honesty, and more, then the results often won't matter and be remembered.

I believe that honesty is an important aspect in our lives whether at work or home. It feels often that it is overlooked.

Often times it may feel as less hurtful to skirt the truth or not be as open as one should. Long term that will hurt the relationship.

Being open and honest with each other lets us know where we stand as well as where we can improve if it is truly constructive and not hurtful.

Not hiding information also allows transparency and trust among each other.

We are all human and we all do mess up from time to time. Raising a hand, reaching out and asking for help to fix the problem and find a way to correct and prevent a reoccurrence should be the way to go. Don't hide it or it will happen again and could be worse.

Let's talk the elephant in the room.

It could any number of things at any given time, but for this discussion let's talk Quality.

In an ideal world a business will have the employees, along with leadership, directly involved in Quality. They would establish the processes and systems needed to do or make the client/customer requirements, then implement, monitor and finally work on continuous improvement.

That is not what usually occurs, so there is a Quality rep or team involved in those steps, working with Process Owners. Sometimes there is no Quality at all in the business, which leaves the business at risk.

Quality easily becomes the elephant in the room, those involved sometimes ostracized within a business, especially when they bring issues to attention that need fixed.

Open, honest and transparent communication is needed within a business to ensure they are meeting their client/customers' requirements at all time. Don't treat Quality or anyone who is trying to help and improve the business as the elephant in the room.

Summary

How do you wish to be perceived by others through your actions? Some may say they don't care, so their actions mean little to them. I would hope that the majority would prefer going down the path that leads to positivity and treating others the right way through honestly, truthfulness, openness and transparency.

We will all be held accountability at some point in our lives for our actions, one way or another. Which path will you take?

Closing

Here we are, at the end. I hope you enjoyed my thoughts on Quality, Business and Life. My goal is to pass knowledge from experience, learn more and continue to grow and learn through life. If you took anything here as a positive, pass it along to those around you.

Change often happens one person, one moment, one action at a time.

Next are some final thoughts.

With me, you get what you see.

My 30+ years of work history since my pre-teens is here, with all the extra things I have done over those years and continue to do. I don't hide or exaggerate what I have done like others may.

I don't put on a facade in my posts across social media. I educate based on my experience and knowledge I have learned in my life.

One thing that has changed in recent years is that people want reality. Regular people posting regular stuff.

While it is okay to want to attain certain things in life, the glamorous posts from various stars and athletes often fall flat to most of society.

Also some top level gurus, whether in finance or other medias don't often give advice based on the real world, but from yesteryear. I see posts online like this all the time.

Each of us is different with different paths in life. What we do, how we do it will be different. What we like will be different. That is okay. That is what makes a diverse world.

In our lives we will do many great things either at work or in our personal lives, even in small ways.

It maybe to help someone through volunteering or other contributions, help someone sick or in difficult times, create systems or products that benefit the company we work for as well as the client/customer.

Most of us may not be at the world stage level to help mass amounts of people, but even one person helped is a positive for both them and you.

The situation I have seen and still see is that often those contributions are forgotten down the road.

Your good deed or good work is forgotten and you either get treated as though you never helped in the first place, or you are tossed aside when you are no longer seen as needed.

In either case you know what you did and that is what is important.

Those who don't forget are the true gems and passing it forward to help others in life will continue to make the world better, one person at a time.

Our legacy is our deeds done while we are here. Let them be to the benefit of others, not through exploitation or other negative connotations.

Let's make a better world together.

How do you want to be remembered?

We all have good days, bad days and some in between.

We come home tired after work and don't have energy for family. They may not see the best of us as we put our energy in our 8 or 12+ hour day at work and that is not a good situation.

We may not get a good night sleep and come into work less than our best which deteriorates throughout the day.

We may have personal issues that cause us to snap at coworkers or have a bad attitude. A situation at work may impact us and set us on course for a bad day.

Constant negativity, divisiveness, and toxic traits in our lives, especially at work, weigh on our psyche. That alone can be mentally exhausting.

Whether we do our best to keep a positive outlook on things, situations will always find a way to push our mindset into the negative.

Do we want to be remembered as a hard worker? Do we want to be remembered as someone who was less than positive to be around? I very much doubt that. I know I don't.

There are times we may require a change of environment as burn out may not be solved with a day off or a short vacation. Something more may be required.

So how do you want to be remembered? How do you want your eulogy written by those who have known you?

Summary

I hope these pages of thoughts from experience helped even in a small way. As I collect more knowledge, more experience, I might roll out a second collection of thoughts.

Feel free to follow me across social media and send your thoughts, ideas and opinions there as we all have much to learn from each other. Always keep it civil. There is not enough civility in the world. We may not always agree with one another, but we should each respect that we each have opinions that may not always align. That is okay.

Together we make the world a better place to live our lives.

About the Author

JD Buzzard was born and raised in Pittsburgh, PA where he lived for twenty years before moving on to Orlando, Florida.

He currently resides in Kuwait City, Kuwait where he has worked as a contractor for the past 17+ years. In Kuwait is where he met his future wife and where their four children were born.

In the workforce for 30+ years, leadership for 15+ years, with national and international experience; traveling to over three dozen countries for fun and work.

Between work and family, he finds the time to write, which has been a hobby of his for over twenty years.

Additionally, over the last dozen years he has assisted in producing over a hundred independent films, whether short or feature films, tv series and music videos.

www.ingramcontent.com/pod-product-compliance
Lightning Source LLC
Chambersburg PA
CBHW062100220526
45471CB00010B/3548